T0282039

When God Thinks of You He Smiles

365 Daily Devotions

BroadStreet
PUBLISHING

BroadStreet Publishing Group, LLC.
Savage, Minnesota, USA
Broadstreetpublishing.com

When God Thinks of You, He Smiles

9781424568055
9781424568062 (eBook)

Devotional entries composed by Sara Perry.

Typesetting and design by Garborg Design Works | garborgdesign.com
Editorial services by Michelle Winger | literallyprecise.com, Carole Holdahl, and
Natasha Marcellus

Printed in China.

24 25 26 27 28 29 30   7 6 5 4 3 2 1

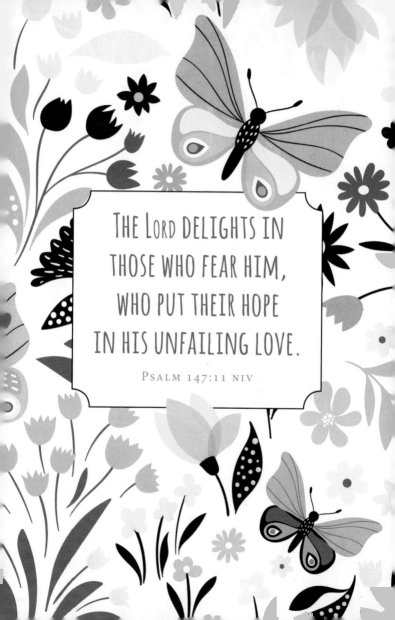

THE LORD DELIGHTS IN
THOSE WHO FEAR HIM,
WHO PUT THEIR HOPE
IN HIS UNFAILING LOVE.

PSALM 147:11 NIV

Introduction

God's love goes infinitely beyond anything you can fathom. You have been adopted into his family, and you are safe in his care. He delights in seeing you walk in truth. Each small step of faith brings him great joy. He created you for relationship with him, and he loves to hear your voice, your laughter, and your thoughts.

As you meditate on these Scriptures, devotions, and prayers, believe that God is also thinking about you. He is not disappointed in you. Nothing about your life is insignificant to him. Ask him to reveal his heart to you and then receive the kindness he so graciously offers. You are on his mind. And he is smiling.

JANUARY

The LORD takes delight in his people;
he crowns the humble with victory.

PSALM 149:4 NIV

WONDERFULLY MADE

I praise you because I am
fearfully and wonderfully made;
your works are wonderful,
I know that full well.

PSALM 139:14 NIV

We were created with intention and thoughtfulness by a loving maker. God took his time crafting our personalities, quirks, and preferences. He relishes his creation! Instead of letting comparison steal our confidence, we should focus on what God says about us. His opinion is what matters most.

God's fingerprints are everywhere, yet you are his greatest masterpiece. There is nothing in creation that God delights in more than you! His affection for you is greater than you can understand. He is not disappointed by you and does not regret creating you. You have a unique and particular purpose in this world. Thank God today for making you just the way you are, for he does not make a single mistake!

My Creator, thank you for making me in your image and thoughtfully knitting me together. Shine the light of your love on me.

JOY OF APPROVAL

Go, eat your bread with joy,
and drink your wine with a merry heart,
for God has already approved what you do.

ECCLESIASTES 9:7 ESV

Every child wants to feel the approval of their parents;
even as adults, we still long for acceptance. It's common to
look at God as though he is constantly disappointed with us.
We fear that he is bothered by our actions and let down by
our poor choices. In reality, God cares more about our hearts
than he does about the little rules we follow. While it is good
to live in a way that is pleasing to him, there is no need to be
enslaved to a list of requirements.

When you have followed God for a long time, certain
behaviors can become almost synonymous with your faith.
As a Christian, you must carefully dance your way through
the balance of living to honor him and knowing that your
actions don't validate your salvation. The key to this dance is
having confidence in God's consistent approval of you. There
is nothing you can do to lessen his acceptance of you.

*Gracious Father, remind me of the power of your love. Please
help me grow in confidence. I want to trust that you approve
of me. Liberate me to walk in courage and delight in what you
have for me today.*

DELIGHT IN HOPE

The LORD's delight is in those who fear him,
those who put their hope in his unfailing love.

PSALM 147:11 NLT

When unforeseen circumstances arise, trusting God's faithfulness may feel challenging. It isn't easy to put our hope in something we cannot see. Yet, the more we depend on the strength of God's love, the more we will experience his delight. Truthfully, there is nothing else worth putting our hope in. Any other person, circumstance, or sense of security will prove unreliable compared to God's love.

Scripture is full of references to God's great love. You can saturate your mind with God's Word when you need a reminder. It assures you that God's love is perfect, strong, and unchanging. Meditate on the truth of God's love today. Let it fill your heart with hope and be your anchor when life is too much to bear. Lean wholeheartedly on the fact that his love will carry you through.

Lord, you delight in those who put their trust in you. When my faith is tested by the trials of this life, help me find security in your unfailing love.

CUES FROM CREATION

By faith we understand that the world has been created by the word of God so that what is seen has not been made out of things that are visible.

HEBREWS 11:3 NASB

As the Creator, God has left his imprint on the world. He set everything in motion initially, and his unfailing love is woven through creation in marvelous ways. When we notice the beauty of nature, we can learn new aspects of God's delight in us. Mysteries of God are revealed when we pay attention to the work of his hands.

Consider the expanse of the sky and the sea, and you will see God's greatness. If you take time to stargaze on a clear night, you will see God's beauty. Observe ecosystems and weather patterns, and you'll see God's intentionality and love of order. You will find so much to marvel at when you take your cues from creation. Let the awe you experience draw you closer to the Creator.

Dear Creator, I often take for granted the natural world around me. Please open my eyes to see all you have done. I want to know you more!

Breakthrough of Love

His love broke open the way,
and he brought me into a beautiful, broad place.
He rescued me—because his delight is in me!

PSALM 18:19 TPT

We've all had relationships that leave us feeling unsteady and insecure. Maybe we disappointed a loved one, or there is distance in a friendship that wasn't there before. It can feel disconcerting to be unsure of where we stand with someone. A lack of security can make us question the validity of the relationship or even our identity as it relates to a specific person. This is never the case in our relationship with God.

You can always be assured of God's great love. There is no need to question if you are secure in it. The power of God's love cannot be overstated. God's mercy and kindness are uninterrupted even when you choose your ways over his. He will gently correct you and never leave you wondering how he feels about you. Take a deep breath and rejoice, knowing you are fully loved and cared for.

Loving Father, even when I question the power of your love, its strength remains the same. Thank you for your unchanging and unfailing love.

God's Creation

Then God saw everything that He had made,
and indeed it was very good.

GENESIS 1:31 NKJV

God created each of us, and he is delighted we are his children. Each of us has been made in his image, reflecting something unique about his character. When we despise what he has done, we miss the enjoyment that comes from reveling in his excellent work. God doesn't focus on our faults and flaws when he looks at us. He sees his beloved children and the work of his love.

When you accept the fullness of God's love, you align yourself with how God sees you. It is not prideful to know that God enjoys you. You are not haughty if you are confident of his love for you. It is good and right for you to experience God's delight in you. Let the light of his love shine on you and give you a sense of security and belonging.

Great God, the strength of your love is almost too much for me to comprehend. Help me lay down any feelings of insufficiency. Reveal your thoughts about me and help me be confident in what you say.

INCOMPARABLE KINDNESS

"If people want to brag, let them brag
that they understand and know me.
Let them brag that I am the LORD,
and that I am kind and fair,
and that I do things that are right on earth."

JEREMIAH 9:24 NCV

God is just and fair; he does not play favorites. God is
astonishingly kind and merciful. He does not seek revenge.
He is not petty, nor is he impatient. He is so gentle and tender
toward his people. These characteristics give God greater
bragging rights than we will ever have. When we indeed
observe who God is, we will quickly realize that there is no
comparison between his perfection and our great weakness.

If you want something to brag about today, brag
about the goodness of God! It is the only thing with true
significance and eternal value in your life. Every good gift
comes from him, and his kindness has no limits. When your
boast is anchored to the perfection of his character, you will
not be disappointed. God is worthy of all your praise.

*Lord, you are better than anyone I've ever known. No one else
compares to you, and I am in awe of all you've done. It's such
a gift to belong to you.*

ALIVE IN CHRIST

God, who is rich in mercy, because of his great love that he
had for us, made us alive with Christ even though we were
dead in trespasses.

EPHESIANS 2:4-5 CSB

Christ's resurrection means we can be fully alive. We
were never meant to be bound to sin and trapped by death.
God's mercy has set us free from bondage and given us the
life for which we were intended. From the beginning, God
desired us to stay in his presence, constantly experiencing
his love and affection.

Scripture reminds you there is no fear in love. You have
nothing to fear in God's assessment of you. He sees you fully
and constantly with eyes of mercy. You are freed from the
fear of punishment. His life-giving love leads to being truly
alive no matter where you are or what you are experiencing.

*Jesus, thank you for the freedom and life you offer me. It is
more than I could ever ask for or imagine. A simple thank you
isn't enough! I can never repay you for your great mercy.*

Hopeful Hearts

The LORD is good to those whose hope is in him,
to the one who seeks him.

LAMENTATIONS 3:25 NIV

God's goodness is our anchor. We can depend on it no matter how stormy life becomes. We can rely on his character because he has proven himself trustworthy. In the face of chaos, confusion, and tragedy, we can stay steady and grounded. The Lord is a loving shepherd and gracious defender. He does not abandon us in our time of need!

God always keeps his promises. He says that he will be good to those whose hope is in him. You can rely on what he says. As you seek him, he is with you. As you trust in his plans for your life, he will keep you safe and on the right path. Lean on him, and he will be faithful to you. When doubt comes knocking, keep your eyes trained on the one who is eternally good.

Lord, you are my hope, and I rely on you for all I need. Your presence is my plentiful portion and my strength. Thank you!

Power of Understanding

May you have the power to understand,
as all God's people should, how wide, how long,
how high, and how deep his love is.

Ephesians 3:18 nlt

God's love cannot be measured. It is greater than our minds can comprehend. It is wider, longer, higher, and deeper than anything we have ever known. Even so, God gives us glimpses of the expanse of his love. His Spirit gives us the power to understand even though our understanding is incomplete. If we stretch our imaginations to the limit, we still will not come close to grasping the fullness of his love.

Instead of measuring God's love according to your perceptions and limitations, you can confidently remove every boundary you have created. As you unravel your expectations, you will see God's love in places you might not have noticed before. Today, ask the Holy Spirit to give you a deeper understanding of how God sees you.

God, I want to understand the greatness of your love! Expand my awareness of your goodness and give me glimpses of your love today.

Pleased By Faith

Without faith it is impossible to please him, for whoever would draw near to God must believe that he exists and that he rewards those who seek him.

Hebrews 11:6 esv

Faith leads us to fellowship with the Almighty. It is through faith that we acknowledge what we cannot see. We trust God because we believe he is worthy of our praise. We believe he is who he says and will be faithful to his promises.

It's so wonderful that to please God, you must simply trust. You don't have to accomplish a long list of to-dos or chase traditional success. You please God because you have put your faith in him. He doesn't care about what you do nearly as much as he cares about your heart. Let this truth bring you freedom and security today.

You are my God, and I believe in you. Open the eyes of my heart to see more of your mercy. I trust that you are pleased with my faith.

Cloak of Kindness

May the kindness of the Lord our God be upon us;
And confirm for us the work of our hands;
Yes, confirm the work of our hands.

PSALM 90:17 NASB

We can be assured of success when God is involved in our work. However, success isn't always linear, and it is rarely immediate. We should keep this in mind as we work. How we gauge success differs from how the world gauges it. God does not promise that we will be wealthy or free from trials in this life. He promises we will have all we need, and he will be with us through everything.

Invite God into the work of your hands. Everything you do is an opportunity to further your relationship with him. Instead of getting caught up in the to-dos of your day, remember that your primary objective is to glorify God. Let him set the standard of success in your life. You'll surely find that he will give you peace and unshakeable confidence in exchange.

Good Father, you are kind in all your ways. Thank you for your persistent presence. I commit my work to you and ask for your constant wisdom to guide me.

OVERSEEN

The Lord sees all we do;
he watches over his friends day and night.
His godly ones receive the answers they seek
whenever they cry out to him.

PSALM 34:15 TPT

What incredible promises we can hold on to as children of the Most High! When we submit our lives to the Lord, we can trust his faithful love to cover us in all we do. He watches over us, helping us whenever we cry to him. Nothing is hidden from God's sight. He sees every problem and knows exactly what we need to overcome it.

God's resources are never depleted. This is true about his character as well. He never runs out of goodness to share with his children. He is patient, kind, and trustworthy. You know what it's like to grow weary and overwhelmed. God, on the other hand, is not bound by our physical and emotional restraints. He has an abundance of kindness to offer whenever you turn to him. You can trust his faithful love to meet you where you are today.

Lord, I can trust you in everything. You do not overlook me. You see my weaknesses and my strengths. Fill me with your love as I open my heart before you.

BEAMING WITH JOY

God be merciful to us and bless us,
And cause His face to shine upon us.

PSALM 67:1 NKJV

Every day is a good day to offer our hearts to the Lord. We can pray consistently, worship unhindered, and serve him wholeheartedly. As we direct our attention to him, he will bless us repeatedly. When we ask the Lord to be merciful to us, we can trust that he will do it. We can approach him confidently because it is his delight to shine upon his children.

God watches over you like a loving father. He delights in giving you good gifts that fill you with joy. Today, spend some time dwelling on the goodness of your heavenly Father. Bask in the satisfaction that comes from knowing you are fully loved. Let his presence wash over you and revive the tired or broken parts of your heart. Receive his blessings with thanksgiving and remember that every good gift comes from his hands.

Father, thank you for the wonders of your love and the mercy you have freely given me. You have blessed me beyond measure and are worthy of my praise.

Chosen

You are a chosen people, royal priests, a holy nation, a people for God's own possession. You were chosen to tell about the wonderful acts of God, who called you out of darkness into his wonderful light.

1 PETER 2:9 NCV

God is light, and in him, all is illuminated. He has called us out of confusion, shame, and insecurity to be rooted in the truth of who he says we are. Our value is not found in what we can offer him but in who he created us to be. We don't have to do anything to earn his love. We can rest in the strength of his mercy.

Consider the powerful truth that God chose you to be his before the foundations of the world were created. Reflect on how that makes you feel. Your true identity is found in how God sees you. Your opinions of yourself are far less important than you may think. As you gain confidence in who God says you are, you will find that your heart, life, and perspective are transformed.

God, thank you for choosing me to be in your family. Reassure me of your love for me. I want to trust what you say about me.

All Things

Everything was created by him, in heaven and on earth,
the visible and the invisible,
whether thrones or dominions or rulers or authorities—
all things have been created through him and for him.

COLOSSIANS 1:16 CSB

When we realize that all things were created through God and for God, we can be more prepared to participate in the delights of this life. We don't have to trudge through the responsibilities of our day. We were made to live, not just to survive. We were made to feast in times of abundance and to celebrate in times of joy! Let's not neglect the power of delight to refresh our hearts and draw us closer to our Creator.

There are so many inescapable trials and sorrows in this life. Relishing the simple joys of your day does not diminish the validity of your frustrations. Delight can refresh your heart and strengthen your resilience. Don't neglect the practice of gratitude or stop noticing little glimmers of hope. Recognize the invitation to praise God for all the goodness you find amidst the messiness of life.

My Creator, thank you for the reminder that life is not meant to be all drudgery. You are so creative in your expressions throughout creation, and I delight in the simple joys I already have at my fingertips.

Hopeful Plans

"For I know the plans I have for you," declares the LORD,
"plans to prosper you and not to harm you, plans to give you
hope and a future."

JEREMIAH 29:11 NIV

Life isn't easy, to be sure. It's not all blooming fields, lush pastures, and sunny days. There are challenging seasons, raging storms, and unforeseen obstacles. Still, God is with us through it all. Nothing surprises him. The power of today's verse rings true even on our darkest days. As we follow him, he will provide everything we need for each varying season.

No matter what disappointments you have experienced, you can be sure that God's plans for you are full of life-giving hope. There is always more ahead. His mercies bring fresh starts, and his grace offers renewed strength. Whatever you need, you can rest in the confidence of God's provision. There is nothing for which he doesn't account. You can trust him in every season!

Faithful One, help me trust your plans more than my own. I take comfort in the fact that nothing surprises you.

Stand Forever

The counsel of the LORD stands forever,
the plans of his heart to all generations.

PSALM 33:11 ESV

God is constant and unwavering. His wisdom does not change over time. Everything about him is precisely the same as it has always been. He is the definition of perfection and the embodiment of reliability. No matter how wild and unpredictable the world seems, God is steady. Governments rise and fall. Natural disasters change the face of the earth, and we experience varying seasons in our own lives. Through it all, God is the same.

When everything in your world feels shaken, God is steady. When you don't know which way is up or how to move forward, God is secure. When you feel like you might be overcome by the darkness or lost in the storm, lean into the shelter of his presence. He never changes, and his counsel is always reliable. He is your rock and your safe place.

God, thank you for being so steady. It's a relief to know that your counsel will stand forever. I trust in your plans because everything you do is good.

Working Together

God causes everything to work together for the good of
those who love God and are called according to his purpose
for them.

ROMANS 8:28 NLT

We are under his care and leadership when we yield
our lives to Christ. This isn't an excuse to do whatever we
want without considering the consequences. Being under
his leadership means we can confidently walk through
our days knowing he is always with us. We can be sure
of God's gracious strength to help us rebuild or repair
when we stumble. Even our most significant failures aren't
intimidating with God on our side.

God is at work in the details of your life. Not everything
you experience seems good, but God does not waste any
moment of your life. He restores the broken things beyond
your ability to mend them. He sows his mercy and grace
into every fiber of your being. If you find yourself in need
of drastic help, don't be dismayed! God will weave his love
through every vulnerable area. You can trust him.

*Gracious God, give me eyes to see where your mercy is at work
in the rubble. My life is imperfect, but your love constantly
teaches me. Thank you.*

First Things First

"Seek first His kingdom and His righteousness,
and all these things will be provided to you."

Matthew 6:33 NASB

If we want to live in the fullness of all God has planned for us, we must seek him first. When we seek the kingdom of God, we put our relationship with him at the forefront of our lives. We adopt God's character and values and let him transform our lives. To do this, we have to know what God is really like. We can find the truth of God's nature within the faithfulness of his character and in his Word.

Responsibilities in life cannot be ignored. Your relationships and commitments require attention and effort. God is aware of your schedule and knows what you must accomplish each day. Seeking him is not just one more thing to add to your list. Instead, let his presence be woven into your day. Lean on him and trust that he will lead you well.

God, I choose to seek you and your values first. The details of my life will come together as I walk in your wisdom. I look to you today, and I trust your faithfulness.

GOD WILL

"I know that You can do everything,
And that no purpose of Yours
can be withheld from You."

JOB 42:2 NKJV

There is nothing that God can't do. His ability is beyond our understanding. With this in mind, let's not withhold a single prayer or request from him. We can be assured that he hears us. He cares about the things we care about. This does not mean every prayer will be answered as expected, but God's faithfulness is unwavering.

Is there something you have kept hidden in your heart, not even sharing with your closest friends? Perhaps you can take it to God today. He will understand even when no one else does. He sees you; he knows you, and he tends to you. Ask him what he thinks and take time to listen. You may be surprised by the kindness of his answer.

Father, you are trustworthy and true. In vulnerability, I bring my hopes to you. Please speak to me and give me grace to listen.

EVERY SINGLE MOMENT

Every single moment you are thinking of me!
How precious and wonderful to consider
that you cherish me constantly in your every thought!

PSALM 139:17 TPT

There isn't one moment when we are hidden from God. He is thinking about his children every single second. What a wonderful mystery! Our heavenly Father thinks of each of us at the same time. He thoughtfully cares for us even more attentively than the perfect parent. He cherishes each of us and is delighted by who he created us to be.

You don't have to do anything to earn your Father's attention or affection. You already have it! With that powerful truth emboldening your heart, you are free to live abundantly as his child. Let his great love impact every area of your life and give you confidence in your true identity. God is with you every single moment of your life.

Father, I cannot begin to comprehend the power of your affection. Still, I'm so glad I have it! Shine on me today. Encourage my heart with hope as I live in the light of your love.

Full of Mercy

You, O Lord, are a God full
of compassion, and gracious,
Longsuffering and abundant in mercy and truth.

PSALM 86:15 NKJV

On difficult days with no silver lining, God's fullness is still present. Our emotions don't dictate God's nature. This is wonderful news! Our foul moods and pessimistic attitudes don't change who God is. When we are hard-pressed to find beauty in challenging circumstances, his beauty remains. God is full of patience, abundant mercy, and wise truth, no matter what hardships we face or the complexity of our emotional reactions to them.

What do you need from God today? Perhaps you need a dose of compassion. He's got it! Maybe you need grace to strengthen you to accomplish what you need to do. He's got that, too! Whatever you require, God's fullness is ready to meet you right where you are. Today, remember that he is always available and able to help you.

Merciful God, thank you for your unchanging nature. Your wisdom and faithfulness are unending. Please fill me up with the power of your presence today.

DWELL IN LOVE

"I loved you as the Father loved me.
Now remain in my love."

JOHN 15:9 NCV

Everything Jesus did on Earth reflected the Father. They are in perfect alignment in thought, word, and deed. If we want to know more about the Father, we simply need to look at Jesus. When we see him, we see God. As such, we can be sure that the way Christ loved others is the same way God loves. We are called to remain in that steady love.

What does it mean to remain in God's love? On a practical level, it means staying in communion with God and honoring his instructions. You can display your love for him by listening to what he says and seeking to remain in his presence. You can worship, thank him for all he's done, and actively live in a way that honors him. Find true satisfaction in his presence and rejoice in his good work. Let him shower you with affection and fill your heart with his love.

Lord, thank you for the power of your love. I choose to follow you for all my days. May your love motivate everything I do. Thank you for the acceptance and satisfaction I find in your presence.

Let Love Reign

Dear friends, let us love one another, because love is from God, and everyone who loves has been born of God and knows God.

1 JOHN 4:7 CSB

It is easy to say we love each other. The words aren't difficult to say, and they feel nice to hear. It is another thing entirely to align our actions with those words. It can be challenging to love consistently in our day-to-day interactions. Scripture tells us that love is patient and kind. It does not envy or boast. It is not arrogant or rude to others. It does not promote its own ways above others, and it rejoices in the truth. It does not harbor resentment, nor does it easily get riled up.

Consider what God's love looks like and let that impact the way you treat others. Scripture gives you a clear picture of how to do this. It is not complicated, though it certainly isn't easy. The good news is that the Holy Spirit can empower you to love like God loves. As you follow him and mature in your understanding of God's great love, it will surely overflow to those around you.

God, I want to love the people around me the way you love me. I know I won't do it perfectly, but I can still choose to be more like you in my relationships. Show me the way and help me honor you.

Extravagant Grace

You have experienced the extravagant grace of our Lord
Jesus Christ, that although he was infinitely rich, he
impoverished himself for our sake, so that by his poverty, we
become rich beyond measure.

2 Corinthians 8:9 tpt

God held nothing back in order to bring us to himself.
He sent his Son to embrace humanity so we can know what
the Father is really like. Jesus Christ broke down every
barrier that was standing between us and God. We are rich
because he chose to become poor. We can have an abundant
life because of the power of his resurrection.

Jesus loves you extravagantly and showers you with
unending grace. His love is not exclusive or bound by
limitations. Christ's love is abundant and unhindered. He
intentionally sacrificed himself, knowing the suffering he
would experience, so that you could experience the goodness
of God. As you meditate on this today, let it lead you to
deeper fellowship with your Maker.

*Faithful One, thank you for the power of your grace and your
extravagant love. Give me a greater understanding of what
you've done for me.*

Called by Grace

He has saved us and called us to a holy life—
not because of anything we have done
but because of his own purpose and grace.

2 Timothy 1:9 niv

What does it mean to live a holy life? God is perfect and holy. Mercy and justice compel him. He is faithful in truth and patient in kindness. He leads with peace and gives abundant grace. Whatever we need is found in him. Holiness is not a stringent list of things to do or behaviors to resist. Rather, it is the effort to reflect the nature of our God.

You are a child of God. You cannot earn your way into his kingdom. The only way in is to accept the grace that he offers you. As you live by the freedom of his grace, you answer the call of holiness. You are worthy to be part of God's kingdom because of what Jesus did for you. He is the one who makes you holy. Today, you can rest knowing that there is nothing you can do to strive for holiness other than depend on the grace given to you.

Lord Jesus, thank you for the grace of your salvation. I am overwhelmed by the gravity of this gift. Keep me from striving and help me rest in what you've already done.

Gift of Grace

By grace you have been saved through faith. And this is not your own doing; it is the gift of God, not a result of works, so that no one may boast.

EPHESIANS 2:8-9 ESV

God's gift of grace is free. It is given unreservedly to all who choose to receive it. It is an abundant offering to everyone. We don't get to decide who is worthy and who isn't. God's grace is the great equalizer. There is no one who deserves an extra portion, and no one is excluded from the deal. We have all fallen short and are all in desperate need of grace.

God is incredibly generous and has an abundance of grace. He does not withhold it from you and does not wait for you to improve yourself before you can receive it. There is nothing you can do to obtain more than you've already been given. The exact portion you need is always available. None of your good deeds are part of the equation. All you can do is humbly accept God's gift.

God, I celebrate your generosity! Thank you for the gift of grace. Help me remain humble and aware of my weaknesses. I don't want to take advantage of the grace you've given me.

Boldly Come

Let us come boldly to the throne of our gracious God.
There we will receive his mercy, and we will find grace
to help us when we need it most.

HEBREWS 4:16 NLT

We all have relationships that are more comfortable than others. We have people who get a more guarded version of ourselves, and we have people we share with freely. We don't wonder what they'll think about us because we trust the strength of the relationship. We're not worried about offending them, and we don't need to walk on eggshells. In the same way, we can approach God without worry or fear. We don't have to tiptoe through our relationship with him.

No matter how formal your thoughts are about God, it is never too late to know him as your confidante and closest friend. He is not strict or overly serious. He delights in you, and he has all the wisdom you need to help you through your struggles. He is a faithful God, quick to listen and slow to anger. Go quickly and boldly into his presence today, for he welcomes you with open arms!

Father, I want to know your grace in deeper ways. Keep me from being anxious or wary in your presence. I want to come to you boldly and with confidence at all times.

God's Child

See how great a love the Father has given us, that we would
be called children of God; and in fact we are.

1 JOHN 3:1 NASB

The way we view ourselves impacts the way we act.
We've all met people who are prideful and boisterous. They
think highly of themselves, and as a result, they feel free to
act however they like. As believers, the same concept should
apply to our lives. We should be unwaveringly aware of who
we are, and it should impact every part of our lives.

It is not presumptuous for children of God to stand
with complete confidence in their identity. It is not prideful
to know who you are. When your identity is secure, your
actions will accurately reflect that knowledge. As God's child,
you are a wonderful creation. You are valuable, and you are
wanted. You belong in his family, and you have a secure
position in his kingdom. There is a place for you at his table.

*Heavenly Father, show me what it truly means to be your
child. Thank you for the freedom of your grace and the
privilege of belonging to you! I want your love to impact every
part of my life.*

Everlasting Life

"God so loved the world that He gave His only begotten Son,
that whoever believes in Him should not perish but have
everlasting life. For God did not send His Son into the world
to condemn the world, but that the world through Him
might be saved."

JOHN 3:16-17 NKJV

Just because we've heard a passage multiple times
shouldn't cause us to overlook it. Perhaps certain parts of
Scripture have become dull to our minds and hearts because of
how often they are used. We tend to skim over the basics of the
gospel when, in reality, they should have the most poignant
impact on our lives. The simple truth is incredibly powerful.
When we return to those familiar verses with open hearts and
fresh eyes, we can re-engage with them in new ways.

Take a moment and ask God to give you a fresh
revelation of today's passage. Remember that as a follower
of Jesus, your entire life is based on the truth found in John.
God loved the world so much that he willingly sacrificed his
son to save it. Not only that, but Jesus saved the world and
then offered unending grace and abundant life to everyone.
Let this truth sink into the depths of your heart.

*Jesus, thank you for coming to set me free. I want to learn
about you and your ways. Help me not to overlook the
glorious simplicity of the gospel.*

February

When doubts filled my mind,
your comfort gave me renewed
hope and cheer.

PSALM 94:19 NLT

Matchless Love

"The greatest love a person can show
is to die for his friends."

JOHN 15:13 NCV

Love is not just a strong emotion toward others. It compels us to act, and it costs something. We may like people well enough in our own strength, but true love requires sacrifice. Love that is impactful is marked by giving up our time, energy, conveniences, money, or preferences. We cannot love fully and remain selfish. The best example of this is the life of Christ and his subsequent death. True, sacrificial, and servant-hearted love is perfectly displayed by what Jesus did.

While you may never physically die for someone else, you can embody Christ's love by being willing to put the needs of others before your own. Look for opportunities to value others more than yourself. God will be faithful in taking care of you so you can elevate others without abandon. When you love in this way, you reflect the perfect love of Christ.

Lord Jesus, your love is not stagnant or silent. You gave your life willingly and without complaint. Help me love in the same sacrificial way.

Place to Hide

O God, how extravagant is your cherishing love!
All mankind can find a hiding place
under the shadow of your wings.

PSALM 36:7 TPT

Our culture might elevate individual strength, but God doesn't. He constantly reminds us that it is good to lean on him. We aren't expected to navigate life on our own. The pressure we feel to have everything figured out all the time isn't from God. We can let go of everyone else's expectations and find peace in his presence.

Have you ever had a day when you just wanted to hide? Perhaps the pressures of life felt like too much, or you just couldn't get a handle on your emotions. This doesn't make you a failure. When you want to run away, hide yourself in God. It is his delight to provide you with shelter from life's storms. He will never shame you or make you feel less than. Instead, he welcomes you into his peaceful and loving presence.

God, I want to run into your presence. Thank you for providing me with shelter and safety. Strengthen me by your Spirit and renew me with your extravagant love.

A Sure Hope

This hope will not disappoint us, because God's love has been poured out in our hearts through the Holy Spirit who was given to us.

ROMANS 5:5 CSB

Our greatest hope doesn't lie in what we can accomplish in this lifetime. Goals are good, and challenging ourselves has merit, but our hope cannot come from our own success. According to the Word, true hope comes only from God. It doesn't diminish or expand based on our own goodness or achievements. We don't get to be hopeful when everything is going our way and then be distraught when trials arise.

When your hope comes from God, it will be unwavering and unshakeable. It won't matter what your outward circumstances are. Your confidence will be steady because you know that even on your worst days, perfection is in the future. God's love has already been poured out through his Spirit. You've experienced his love and can trust that if you put your hope in him, you won't be disappointed. He will faithfully keep all his promises.

Holy Spirit, pour the endless love of God into my heart today. Refresh my hope and help me follow you faithfully no matter what difficulties I face.

Rich Provider

Command those who are rich in this present world not
to be arrogant nor to put their hope in wealth, which is so
uncertain, but to put their hope in God, who richly provides
us with everything for our enjoyment.

1 Timothy 6:17 niv

The favor of God is not seen in our bank accounts. It
isn't found in the treasuries of this world. It is far greater
than earthly wealth, which comes and goes so easily. God is
the God of the poor, the outcast, and the broken. He is the
watcher of the widows and the caretaker of the orphans. He
is close to the broken-hearted, and he comforts those who
have had great loss.

If you find yourself wealthy by the world's standards,
you have the responsibility to align yourself with God's
heart. Commit your finances to him with humility and ask
him for wisdom. Seek to use your resources to bless others.
Remember that wealth isn't the most important thing in
your life. In seasons of plenty and in seasons of want, you are
called to put your hope primarily in God.

*Generous One, may I never withhold help when I'm able to
give it. May I always put my hope in you and not in what I do
or don't have. You are my provider, and I trust you.*

Display His Glory

We are his workmanship, created in Christ Jesus
for good works, which God prepared beforehand,
that we should walk in them.

EPHESIANS 2:10 ESV

You were created with a purpose. As an expression of
God's goodness, you were made to display his glory. You
were made in his image, and you are a living reflection of
his love. Everything he has prepared for you is good. He is
endlessly creative and kind. As long as you are living, there
are opportunities to experience his restorative power and
redemptive mercy!

Nothing in your life is too hard for God to overcome. No
wound is beyond his healing power. Trust him because he
knows you better than anyone else. You are his workmanship
and the delight of his heart. Walk in his ways and follow in
his footsteps. His path for you is full of life and hope.

*Jesus, thank you for the power of your mercy in my life. No
problem is too big for you to handle. Help me walk in your
ways and reflect your goodness to the world around me.*

BLAMELESS

Now he has reconciled you to himself through the death of
Christ in his physical body. As a result, he has brought you
into his own presence, and you are holy and blameless as you
stand before him without a single fault.

COLOSSIANS 1:22 NLT

Christ is our covering. His sacrifice cleanses us of our
insufficiencies and makes us whole. We have been reconciled
to God through his death. There is no more shame or
condemnation for those who are surrendered to Jesus. We
are liberated in his love and can stand confidently in his
grace. There is nothing we can do to earn this position.
Instead, we must accept that it is undeserved yet given freely.

In God's eyes, you are blameless. You are covered by
the blood of the Lamb and are considered without fault.
When God looks at you, he does not see your mistakes or
your failures. He doesn't keep track of how many times you
mess up, even if it's the same thing over and over. He is not
disappointed by you, and he is not ashamed. You have laid
your life down at the cross, and he is overjoyed to welcome
you into his family.

*Jesus, thank you for the power of your love, which sets me
free from blame. You are amazing, and I rejoice in your
overwhelming goodness. Help me see myself the way you do.*

Tremendous Blessings

Praise be to the God and Father of our Lord Jesus Christ,
who has blessed us in the heavenly realms with every
spiritual blessing in Christ.

EPHESIANS 1:3 NIV

When we come to understand the wealth of God's
love and all that he freely pours over his children, our
capacity for gratitude grows. We can only respond with
thanksgiving when we realize that the abundant resources
in God's kingdom are available to us. As followers of Jesus,
we are considered sons and heirs. We will receive the same
inheritance from God that Jesus has. Our place in the
kingdom is secure, and we will spend eternity enjoying the
fullness of God's presence.

For a brief time, Adam and Eve experienced fellowship
with God the way it was intended to be. There isn't supposed
to be anything standing in the way of perfect, uninterrupted
communion with your Maker. While sin once separated
you from God, now you are redeemed because of Christ's
death. Jesus made a way for you to experience every good
thing that God has to offer. Because of Jesus, every spiritual
blessing is yours.

Lord, thank you for Christ's sacrifice. When I am discouraged,
remind me of the redemption and liberation I get to enjoy.

Just Like Him

As those who have been chosen of God, holy and beloved,
put on a heart of compassion, kindness, humility, gentleness,
and patience.

Colossians 3:12 nasb

As followers of Jesus, we are meant to be compassionate,
kind, humble, gentle, and patient. As we emulate these
qualities, we reflect God's love for the people around us.
Though we live in a world that edifies being independent,
selfish, prideful, and vain, we are meant to behave differently.
In light of Christ's sacrifice, we set aside our own ambitions
and instead seek to share God's love with the world.

Loving others is not meant to be one more thing you
need to accomplish. There's no need to feel shame if you are
struggling to embody the character traits listed in today's
Scripture. Instead, remember that as you follow the Holy
Spirit's leading, he will cause fruit to grow in your life. You
may not wake up one day and be fully compassionate or
patient, but God will provide you with opportunities to
gently teach you each day.

*Lord Jesus, thank you for the beauty and power of your
character. I want my character to look like yours. Show me
how I can grow in kindness and humility. I want to honor you
with my actions.*

He Rejoices

"He will rejoice over you with gladness,
He will quiet you with His love,
He will rejoice over you with singing."

ZEPHANIAH 3:17 NKJV

When we catch a glimpse of God's heart, we may be surprised to see how much joy he has toward us. He delights in his children! He is a mighty God who saves valiantly, and he is a compassionate Father who loves perfectly. He does not harbor any indignation toward his creation. He is strong, powerful, and sovereign, and he is so happy we are his.

No matter what you need today, God can provide it. If you need comfort, he will hold you close. If you need to be rescued, he will be faithful. If you are anxious, he will quiet your heart. Your heavenly Father adores you! You may look at yourself and see vivid examples of your failures, but when he looks at you, he sees you with eyes of mercy and delight. Be refreshed by the abundance of love he pours over you.

God, please give me a greater understanding of your love. In the depths of my soul, I want to believe that I delight you. I praise you for all the ways your love has sustained me.

Day By Day

Just as you accepted Christ Jesus as your Lord, you must continue to follow him. Let your roots grow down into him, and let your lives be built on him.

COLOSSIANS 2:6-7 NLT

Our lives are meant to be built on Jesus. He is supposed to be the foundation for everything we do. Following him does not only impact our eternal salvation. Our everyday lives should reflect the grace we have received so freely. Until the day we see him face to face, we are on a continuous journey to glorify him with the way we live.

Notice that today's scripture says to build your life upon Jesus. It doesn't say you are instantly given a perfect life. You are meant to honor Jesus with your actions, but it is perfectly normal for this to be a process that is done step by step. Strong roots do not grow overnight. Each day, you have the opportunity to experience more of Christ's love than you did the day before.

Jesus, I want my life to be built upon you. Help me grow in love each day. As I follow you, keep my steady. You are my rock and my firm foundation.

TRUE FREEDOM

We have freedom now, because Christ made us free. So stand strong. Do not change and go back into the slavery of the law.

GALATIANS 5:1 NCV

The freedom that Christ gives is not temporary. It is eternal, and it will not diminish in value or efficacy. We are not meant to experience his freedom and then go back to our old habits. He blessed us with generous grace that is ours for eternity. The power of his sacrifice is enough to cover every misstep, mistake, and failure.

True freedom means that you don't have to repeat the patterns of the past. You can forge new pathways in God's love and by his grace. You can walk in his kindness, follow him out of destructive cycles, and experience fresh mercy each day. Stand firmly in who God says you are. He will empower you to choose the liberating way of his love!

Gracious God, I want to live in freedom and confidence. Show me how to rely on the power of your resurrection. Help me choose your mercy and to steadily walk away from my old way of living.

Good Stewards

Just as each one has received a gift, use it to serve others,
as good stewards of the varied grace of God.

1 PETER 4:10 CSB

Everyone has unique talents and gifts. Our strengths can be used to build up the people around us. A good listener can use that ability to encourage and serve others. Someone who loves to make new friends can be great at connecting people and making others feel noticed. No matter how varied they are, each believer has gifts that are given to them by God for the edification of the body.

If you don't know what your gifts are, take time to ask the Lord. He will faithfully show you how you can uniquely serve others. Think about what brings you joy and causes you to feel fulfilled. It is likely that whatever comes to mind is God's gift to you. Whatever it may be, use it for his glory over your own. You were uniquely created to display a specific aspect of the varied grace of God.

My Creator, I know we all have unique strengths, and I am thankful for how you made me. Help me use my strengths to serve and uplift others. I want to glorify you in all I do.

No Separation

I am convinced that neither death nor life, neither angels nor demons, neither the present nor the future, nor any powers, neither height nor depth, nor anything else in all creation, will be able to separate us from the love of God that is in Christ Jesus our Lord.

ROMANS 8:38-39 NIV

Nothing can separate us from the love of God. There is great security to be found in this truth. God's love is always with us. Even if we wander away by our own volition, we can always turn back toward God's love. Darkness cannot consume us, and death cannot hold us down. There is nothing in the universe that is strong enough to keep God from loving us.

God's love for you is greater than you can fathom. You can rely on it in all circumstances. You can trust him to lead you through whatever life throws at you. He will never change the way he thinks about you. Nothing you can do will cause him to abandon you or decide that you aren't worth his time. He will never stop pursuing you or giving you opportunities to experience his love.

God, I am so thankful for the greatness of your love. Thank you for being so faithful and consistent in my life. When my mind is flooded with doubts, remind me of the enduring power of your love.

GENTLE AND MIGHTY

You have given me the shield of your salvation,
and your right hand supported me,
and your gentleness made me great.

PSALM 18:35 ESV

God is a mighty warrior and the creator of the universe. We might not typically affiliate those titles with gentleness. God is the full embodiment of everything good. As such, he is perfectly strong, gentle, wise, mighty, kind, and passionate. None of his characteristics contradict each other. When we struggle to understand an aspect of his character, it is simply an invitation to look beyond our human understanding and marvel at his perfection.

Gentleness isn't a quality that is typically praised by society. You may have even wrongly associated it with weakness or passivity. God says that his gentleness will make you great. It is not his power or might that set him apart, though he has those things in abundance. Instead, his kind heart and gentle spirit are what meet you in your weakness. No matter how you've been treated in the past, remember that God desires to be gentle with you.

God, meet me with gentleness, love, and the power of your presence. You are not harsh or unkind. Your sweet patience is what draws me closer to your heart. Thank you for always being gentle with me.

NOT A BURDEN

"Do not be afraid or discouraged, for the Lord will
personally go ahead of you. He will be with you;
he will neither fail you nor abandon you."

DEUTERONOMY 31:8 NLT

The Lord is a trustworthy leader. He is a confident
helper in times of trouble. He is a loyal friend in every
circumstance. We never need to go it alone! When we find
ourselves overwhelmed by the pressures of life, God is a
steady support. He has all the wisdom and strength we need.
He is never confused, and there isn't a challenge that he
cannot overcome.

Instead of letting fear or discouragement lead your
actions today, turn your hearts over to the Lord. Invite him
to lead you. You can follow in his footsteps. He will never
leave you or fail you. He won't abandon you to figure things
out on your own. He is faithful, dependable, always near, and
always available!

*Faithful One, thank you for your constant presence. I'm glad
that I don't have to be alone. I trust you to guide me and
faithfully help me every step of the way.*

Redeemed

He rescued us from the domain of darkness,
and transferred us to the kingdom of His beloved Son,
in whom we have redemption, the forgiveness of sins.

COLOSSIANS 1:13-14 NASB

When we discover the generosity of God's love for us, we find a great and joyous treasure. He rescued us from the tyranny of darkness and gave us new life. We have been redeemed by the blood of the Lamb and are free to spend eternity in the presence of the Father. There is nothing holding us back from experiencing the freedom, joy, and satisfaction that comes from communion with the one who made us.

Surrender your life at the cross and accept the gift of glorious freedom that is being offered to you. You can live in the light just as God is in the light. Lay down your burdens and remember that nothing is big enough to disqualify you from God's mercy. There is no conflict, sin, anxiety, or frustration that changes the truth of what Christ has done for you.

Lord Jesus, in your light of love I come alive. You are the one who has washed away my fear, shame, and guilt. You are my Savior and I worship you!

MOTIVATING FAITH

Faith motivated Abraham to obey God's call and leave the
familiar to discover the territory he was destined to inherit
from God. So he left with only a promise and without even
knowing ahead of time where he was going, Abraham
stepped out in faith.

HEBREWS 11:8 TPT

Faith is an important element in our relationship with
God. We cannot know exactly how tomorrow or any day
in the future will play out, but we can trust that God will
be with us every step of the way. He sees the obstacles
we cannot anticipate. He guides us through unnavigable
situations and encourages us when we are full of despair.
Through faith, we trust that he is with us even when we
cannot see or feel him.

You can faithfully follow God's leadership just like
Abraham did. The faith that motivated Abraham was planted
in him by God himself. Abraham didn't have special skills
or a unique ability to do the right thing. He simply believed
that God was capable and trustworthy. Ask God to lead you
and trust that he will not cause you to misstep. Follow where
he leads you, even when it doesn't make sense.

*Faithful Father, thank you for your faithful leadership in my
life. I will follow your call and trust your steadfast character
with my whole heart.*

TENDER MERCIES

Do not withhold Your tender mercies
from me, O LORD;
Let Your lovingkindness and Your truth
continually preserve me.

PSALM 40:11 NKJV

The Lord is gracious and compassionate. He is slow to
anger, and he abounds in love. When we feel the intensity
of our own weaknesses, we have the opportunity to lean on
the strength of our mighty God. Scripture is full of urgent
prayers and pleas. No matter how many times we stumble,
God faithfully lifts us up and welcomes us into his presence.
We can be honest and authentic before him, and he will not
turn us away. He is a faithful Father.

What do you need from God today? You can go to
him with all you are and all you need. Don't withhold your
honest prayers. There is no need to tidy yourself up before
you call out to him. You don't need to make sense of your
inner self before you run into his arms. The more you turn
your attention to God, the more you will see the greatness
of his mercy. His love is big enough to cover all of your
insufficiencies.

*Lord, I won't keep my feelings hidden from you today. Neither
will I ignore the pressing needs I have which I cannot meet on
my own. Please pour out your tender mercies on my life.*

Trustworthy Support

"Don't worry, because I am with you.
Don't be afraid, because I am your God.
I will make you strong and will help you;
I will support you with my right hand that saves you."

ISAIAH 41:10 NCV

We cannot escape the frustrations of this life. It is wise to lean on the Lord for help and guidance. That is what gives us strength when trials and suffering come our way. Jesus himself didn't avoid hunger, grief, or weakness. The presence of difficulty does not negate the presence of God. Trouble will come to everyone at some point. We don't need a seamless life. What we truly need is a dependency on the eternal faithfulness of the Lord.

When you struggle, it doesn't mean that your faith is lacking. No one is immune to trials. Even when you faithfully follow God, life can still be rocky. His grace is your strength, and his presence is your peace. No matter what your circumstances are, he is with you. Place your confidence in his reliability and Lean on his faithfulness.

Generous One, thank you for the faithfulness of your love, which never leaves me. I don't want to spend my life worrying or full of fear. Empower me and encourage me when I struggle.

Count On Him

Humble yourselves, therefore, under the mighty hand of God,
so that he may exalt you at the proper time, casting all your
cares on him, because he cares about you.

1 PETER 5:6-7 CSB

Scripture confirms that God consistently exalts the
humble. He lifts up, elevates, and encourages those who
recognize their need for him. We cannot trust in his
provision or faithfulness if pride and arrogance are in
our way. When we lay down our pride, acknowledge our
weakness, and admit our need for him, we set ourselves up
for true success.

In a culture that elevates independence and worldly
success, it can be difficult to admit your weakness and
vulnerability. When you acknowledge your inability to save
yourself, you make room for God's strength to be magnified.
He won't use his strength to condemn, punish, or shame you.
He cares about the concerns of your heart, and he is gentle
with the vulnerable issues in your life. You can count on him
to encourage you when you are weak.

*Good Father, you are constant in your care for me. Thank you
for your love and faithfulness. Help me bring my weakness to
you, trusting that you will be glorified in my life.*

Lasting Peace

"Peace I leave with you; my peace I give you. I do not give
to you as the world gives. Do not let your hearts be troubled
and do not be afraid."

John 14:27 niv

The peace of God isn't fragile; it isn't easily lost. God's
peace is dependent on his own character and is therefore
consistent and dependable. Though we may walk on
eggshells for fear of upsetting certain people in our lives, this
never needs to be our approach with God. He is not easily
upset or angered. He is patient, kind, and offers us a peace
that cannot be shaken.

God's peace does not change based on how you feel
or what is going on in your life. It isn't based on external
circumstances or whether or not you deserve it. Embrace
your inability to manufacture peace for yourself and
surrender in the presence of your Maker. Allow him to settle
your heart and calm your fears.

*Lord, I need more of your peace in my life. Thank you for
being consistent and reliable no matter how I feel. Help me
surrender my anxieties and trust in your faithfulness.*

Through It All

"When you pass through the waters, I will be with you;
and through the rivers, they shall not overwhelm you;
when you walk through fire you shall not be burned,
and the flame shall not consume you."

ISAIAH 43:2 ESV

God is with us through every high and low in this life.
Through every trial and every victory, he is our present
companion and faithful helper. He promises that we
will never face anything alone! God was with Shadrach,
Meshach, and Abednego in the fiery furnace. He was with
Daniel in the lion's den, and he was with Moses during the
liberation of his captive people. He was faithful to each of
them, and he will be faithful to us today.

No matter what impossible circumstances you are
facing, God is with you. If you feel like you are drowning,
he offers his hand. If you need a shield from the flames of
adversity, he offers you protection. Remember how God has
been faithful to you in the past, and trust that he will not let
you down today. Through it all, God is with you.

*Faithful One, remind me of how you have delivered me in
the past. Encourage me when I am overwhelmed. I trust your
faithfulness.*

Faithful Caregiver

"That is why I tell you not to worry about everyday life—
whether you have enough food and drink,
or enough clothes to wear. Isn't life more than food,
and your body more than clothing?"

MATTHEW 6:25 NLT

God is a faithful father who delights in caring for his children. All that we need will be provided. This is why Jesus instructed us not to worry about the necessities. God is very aware of what we need. It does not surprise him, and he isn't annoyed by our inability to care for ourselves. He doesn't look at us begrudgingly, and he isn't inconvenienced by our weakness.

Worrying about things you cannot control is a recipe for becoming overwhelmed and discouraged. This is not the way God wants you to live. He wants you to live abundantly, experience freedom, and lean on his provision. He doesn't make promises that he cannot keep. You can let go of your worries and trust that he is fully capable of handling them.

Creator, you are my maker and my provider. You know my needs better than I do. Help me let go of my worries and trust in your ability to care for me.

Overflow

God is able to make all grace overflow to you, so that,
always having all sufficiency in everything, you may have an
abundance for every good deed.

2 CORINTHIANS 9:8 NASB

The generosity of God has no limitations. This is as
true today as it was when God set creation in motion. His
resources never run dry; they are always overflowing. He
is able to satisfy the needs of all living things from the
beginning of creation into eternity. There is no situation that
is too complicated for him to handle. God is able to provide
whatever we need at any given moment.

Do you approach God with hesitancy or confidence? Do
you trust that he is capable and willing to meet your needs?
No matter what your answers are, God remains the same. He
is faithful to you even when your faith is weak. His ability to
provide for you does not depend on the strength of your belief.
Even when you doubt his goodness, his goodness doesn't
change. Let his consistency and reliability bring you peace.

*Generous God, you are overflowing with grace, truth, and
love. Broaden my limited perspective today. I choose to come
to you with the expectation that you will meet my needs.*

Good Guidance

"I will stay close to you,
instructing and guiding you
along the pathway for your life.
I will advise you along the way
and lead you forth with my eyes as your guide."

PSALM 32:8 TPT

God is a good leader. This is not just because he sees every possibility but also because he leads with love. He wants what is best for us, and we can trust him not to lead us astray. He doesn't promise that our lives will be without obstacles, but he does promise to guide us through each one. He is a good, faithful, and trustworthy leader.

Today is full of possibilities. God is close, and he loves you with a deep and loyal love. If you lean on God throughout your day, his presence will wash over you. You will feel the warmth of his affection and hear his gentle voice as he speaks. As you trust in him, he will skillfully guide you through or around each obstacle that comes up. He does not expect you to navigate your life alone. He wants to take each step together.

Good Shepherd, guide me along the pathway of my life. Encourage my heart with your nearness today. I trust you to lead me well.

MADE IN HIS IMAGE

Then God said, "Let Us make man in Our image,
according to Our likeness."

GENESIS 1:26 NKJV

We were each created in the image of God. Every
human is a unique reflection of him. Just like we bear
a resemblance to our earthly parents, we also bear a
resemblance to the Creator. We were created with intricacy,
thoughtfulness, and intention. When we despise parts of
ourselves, we miss the innate sense of belonging that can
be found in understanding our true identity. Loving God's
creation is one way to show love for God himself.

If you struggle to see goodness in yourself, go to the
One who knows you better than anyone else. Ask him to
open your eyes so you can see how you reflect his likeness.
Open your heart to what he says about you, who he created
you to be, and how much he delights in you. If you struggle
to see yourself in a positive light, trust that he will gently
guide you toward an understanding of the truth. You are his
child, and he loves you!

*Father, thank you for creating me with thoughtfulness and
love. Open my eyes and help me see myself as you do. Shine
the light of your truth into my heart and mind until I am
convinced of your love for me.*

LOVE AND HONOR

Love each other like brothers and sisters. Give each other
more honor than you want for yourselves.

ROMANS 12:10 NCV

Jesus showed us what God's love looks like. He listened
to the lonely, healed the sick, and offered wisdom to those
who sought it. He offered friendship to his disciples and
forgave them for their failures. This is how we are meant to
love each other. We honor God when we put the needs of
others before our own. This isn't always easy or convenient,
but it is how we are intended to live.

If honoring others over yourself feels scary or
impossible, consider the reason. You cannot give from an
empty well. If you are depleted and weary, of course, you
won't be able to love others sacrificially. The good news is
that God's love doesn't have limits. Go to him and trust that
he will fill you up. He doesn't expect you to give something
you don't have. Let his love comfort you, cover you, and
bring you peace.

*Lord, I need to experience your love today. Give me grace
to honor those around you more than myself. I want to love
sacrificially and with generosity.*

Draw Near

Lord, keep pouring out your unfailing love
on those who are near you.
Release more of your blessings to
those who are loyal to you.

PSALM 36:10 TPT

Drawing near to God isn't like entering a bank and making a withdrawal. We don't go to him for what we need and then make a quick exit. Instead, our relationship with him is like going to the home of a beloved parent or friend. We walk in the door fully expecting to find a sense of belonging and a desire to stay as long as possible. We seek that relationship for the love, enjoyment, and connection we find there.

If your relationship with God feels stoic, ask him to give you a revelation of his love for you. If your relationship feels cold or transactional, ask him to open your eyes to his great affection for you. He wants you to experience the comfort and familiarity of his presence. He wants you to know him as a kind and beloved father. Let the truth of who God is filter down from your mind and create deep roots in your heart.

Great God, thank you for meeting me with kindness whenever I draw near you. Continue to pour out your love on my life. I want to be delighted to spend time with you.

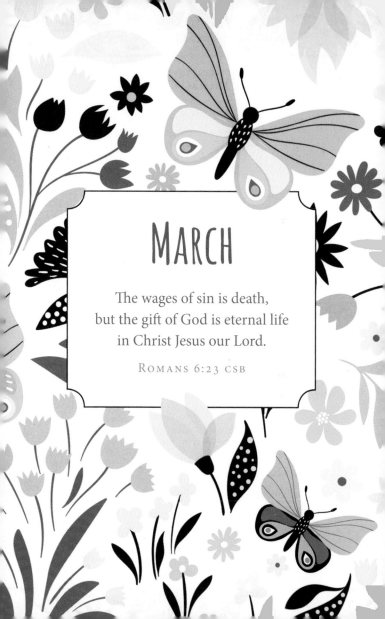

MARCH

The wages of sin is death,
but the gift of God is eternal life
in Christ Jesus our Lord.

ROMANS 6:23 CSB

Sustaining Care

"Don't be afraid;
you are worth more than many sparrows."

Matthew 10:31 csb

God loves and cares for even the smallest creatures. His tender care reaches across all creation. Each living thing plays a part in a bigger system and reflects God's creativity and majesty. He has lovingly ensured that the world is perfectly woven together. He delights in all of creation. As his image bearer, you are at the very top of that list.

If God tends to the smallest sparrow, he will surely take care of you. He knows exactly what you need, and he is fully capable of providing it. He has sustained you this far, and he will continue to do so. Think about the needs he has already met. What joys have you become accustomed to? Soften your heart and try not to overlook the care he has already given. Rejoice in what he has done and wait expectantly for him to meet your future needs.

God, thank you for taking care of me. You see every detail of my life, and you know exactly what I need. Help me trust you instead of dwelling on my fears. I lay my worries at your feet, and I trust you will take care of me.

Overflow with Hope

May the God of hope fill you with all joy and peace as you trust in him, so that you may overflow with hope by the power of the Holy Spirit.

ROMANS 15:13 NIV

As we trust in God, he fills us with joy and peace. We bring him our weakness, and he gives us strength. We give him our feeble attention, and he overwhelms us with goodness. We glance at him, and he is delighted by our gaze. We bring almost laughable levels of devotion, and he fills us to overflowing with hope. His faithfulness is exponentially greater than ours, yet he never holds it over us or makes us feel small for offering him what we have.

Let God fill you with hope. No matter how little you have to give or how far you've wandered from his ways, accept his gift of abundant grace. Turn to him today and begin to trust him again. Reach out to him, and he will meet you. It is never too late to be renewed and restored by your loving Maker.

God of hope, I rely on you! Fill me with joy and peace as I trust in you. Heal my brokenness as I turn to you. Mend what is broken and give me fresh hope for tomorrow.

COMPASSIONATE ONE

"The mountains may depart
and the hills be removed,
but my steadfast love shall not depart from you,
and my covenant of peace shall not be removed,"
says the LORD, who has compassion on you.

ISAIAH 54:10 ESV

We all go through cycles in our relationships and our lives. Not every season is going to be smooth, steady, or easy to navigate. It's normal to experience doubt and frustration. We don't need to be discouraged by the emotions that we construe as negative. God isn't intimidated by our human limitations. He is compassionate toward us in spite of our inability to remain faithful. This is what makes God's faithfulness so life changing.

God is your ready and available helper, especially on days when you just can't seem to get it together. He is with you in the messes as well as in the miracles. Look to him, for he will not withhold his mercy from you. He is a faithful friend and a powerful Savior. His compassion is steadfast, and he will not let you down.

Merciful Father, meet me with the abundance of your compassion today. I need a fresh revelation of your love. Strengthen me where I am weak and help me trust you more.

Love Others

"I have told you these things so that you will be filled
with my joy. Yes, your joy will overflow! This is my
commandment: Love each other in the same way I have
loved you."

JOHN 15:11-12 NLT

Jesus showed us what the Father's love looks like. He
healed the sick, comforted the grieving, and welcomed the
lonely into his family. We are meant to love others in the
same way. As followers of Jesus, we do our best to follow his
example. We can feed the hungry, advocate for the helpless,
and embrace the weary. Not only does loving others point
them to the Father, but it brings us great joy.

Allow God's love to saturate every choice you make. If
you look for opportunities to love people, you will see them
everywhere. There are endless options. Each interaction you
have can point someone to the gracious love of their Maker.
This is not meant to be a burden or an impossible task. It's
a great privilege to be an image bearer of the Lord. If loving
others sounds overwhelming, let God minister to your heart.
He will meet you in your weakness and be glorified by your
willingness to serve.

*God, I want to love others as you have loved me. Renew my
spirit and show me opportunities to serve others. Teach me
how to share your life-giving love with everyone around me.*

Unfailing Mercy

The Lord's acts of mercy indeed do not end,
For His compassions do not fail.
They are new every morning;
Great is Your faithfulness.

LAMENTATIONS 3:22-23 NASB

God never runs out of compassion. His resources don't deplete, and he never hides from us. He is always available, and he is always rich in mercy. Whatever we need, he has it in spades. We don't need to hesitate to run to him because his door is always open. No matter what we look like when we knock, he opens his arms and welcomes us in.

Have you ever been asked what risks you would take if you knew you couldn't fail? In the same way, think about how you would approach God if you knew his compassion would never fail. Truly, there is nothing you can do to generate more mercy from God. He will never tire of loving you. He will never turn you away or get sick of you. He will never be disgusted by your failures or let down by your weaknesses. The enduring love he has for you is deeper than you can imagine.

Faithful God, your kindness and generosity are astounding. Sometimes, I forget how wonderful you are, yet you remain full of compassion. Thank you for always welcoming me into your arms.

Intimately Aware

We have come into an intimate experience with God's love,
and we trust in the love he has for us.
God is love! Those who are living in love are living in God,
and God lives through them.

1 JOHN 4:16 TPT

When we become part of God's family, he becomes
our teacher, father, and friend. As we spend time with him,
we become familiar with his character and the effects of a
relationship with him. Each day, we are transformed into his
likeness. We trust in his promises and rely on his goodness.
We learn to live in a way that pleases him, and we faithfully
follow his plan for our lives.

Your life is meant to be transformed by truth. As you
follow God you will learn to reflect his character more and
more. When you experience the goodness of his love, it will
impact every area of your life. God's love changes the way
you see yourself, the way you see others, and the way you
interact with the world around you. Ask the Holy Spirit
to show you how God's love has impacted you. He will be
faithful and gently guide you.

God, I want to experience more of your life. I want every area
of my life to be impacted by you. Thank you for living through
me as I grow in understanding.

Captivated by Kindness

The LORD has appeared of old to me, saying:
"Yes, I have loved you with an everlasting love;
Therefore with lovingkindness I have drawn you."

JEREMIAH 31:3 NKJV

When God appeared to Jeremiah, he offered hope for restoration to the nation of Israel. God drew his people to him with everlasting love right from the beginning. It is that same love that rebuilds and restores us today. God's love has not changed from the beginning of time up until this very minute. It is our strong foundation, and it gives us hope for the future.

God doesn't appeal to you by making sure you know how weak or broken you are. He doesn't point out your flaws and expect you to come running. He wants to draw you in with lovingkindness. He wants to restore every broken part of your heart. He brought redemption to entire nations, and he wants to redeem you as well. His desire is for you to spend eternity in his presence. He wants to keep you safe and give you hope. Rejoice that his plans for you are good. Go to him with thanksgiving and praise him for all he has done for you.

Everlasting Father, captivate my heart with your kindness once more. Renew my heart with hope as you revive me with your presence today. Thank you!

LIFETIMES OF LOVE

Know that the LORD your God is God, the faithful God.
He will keep his agreement of love for a thousand lifetimes
for people who love him and obey his commands.

DEUTERONOMY 7:9 NCV

God is a covenant keeper. He makes promises and
then perfectly executes them. If he says something, he will
do it. His Word never returns void. It always accomplishes
precisely what he intends. Everything he does is good and
lines up perfectly with his character. We are each part of a
much bigger story of God's love. He has kept his agreement
of love for thousands of generations already and he will
continue to keep it.

How long have you kept a promise? Under the most
extreme circumstances, your answer would still be less than
one hundred years. Your perception of covenants is limited
to your own lifetime. Your understanding of what it means
to be faithful is bound by human understanding. God does
not have limitations. You've seen glimpses of his faithfulness,
but one day, you will clearly see the whole picture. One
day, you will fully grasp what it means for God to keep his
agreement of love with his people forever.

*Unchanging One, your love has no limitations. I am in awe
of your ability to keep your promises. I put my trust in you
because you have proven yourself over and over.*

Poised for Love

May the Lord direct your hearts to God's love
and Christ's endurance.

2 Thessalonians 3:5 csb

God showers us with love, and Jesus teaches us how to endure. With love and endurance, we can run our race well. We can faithfully surrender our lives to God and live in a way that honors him. We can embrace trials because we know that one day, all our tears will be wiped away. God's love fills us, empowers us, and motivates us to be faithful. Christ's life teaches us how to embrace suffering and endure to the very end.

The world may seem darker now than ever, but God is not intimidated. In his love, you have everything you need. When you rely on his love, you will remain steady and secure. He has given you everything you need to stand strong in the face of darkness and temptation. No matter how far society wanders from God's ways, his love and Christ's endurance will carry you to the end.

Lord, fill my heart with your love today. Empower me and give me what I need to endure each day. Guide me through each season of my life. I trust you to keep me steady.

Inner Strength

I pray that out of his glorious riches he may strengthen you
with power through his Spirit in your inner being, so that
Christ may dwell in your hearts through faith.

EPHESIANS 3:16-17 NIV

God wants to strengthen us from the inside out. This,
like many other areas of Scripture, communicates that our
hearts and spirits are more important than our outward
appearances or actions. We are easily distracted by behaviors,
but God is not. He sees into our hearts and would rather lead
us toward inner transformation than outward perfection. He
is far less concerned with our actions than we are.

If you're honest with yourself, do you focus more on
your behavior or the attitude of your heart? Take a deep
breath and stop striving. Let your heavenly Father hold
you and communicate his great approval of you. He loves
you so much. Set aside your desire for perfection and let
the kindness of his heart transform yours. As you find
acceptance in his presence, he will strengthen your inner
being. Then, your actions will begin to reflect what he has
already done in your heart.

*Holy Spirit, strengthen me in my innermost being and
build me up with the power of your love. Thank you for
transforming me from the inside out. Your ways are always
better than mine.*

Better than Life

Because your steadfast love is better than life,
my lips will praise you.

PSALM 63:3 ESV

When we discover something that changes our lives for
the better, we can't help but speak about it. We are quick to
share about a gadget that improved our productivity or a
theory that helped us be more organized. It's easy to share all
the silly ways we see improvement in our lives, yet we often
struggle to share how God's love has transformed us.

The love of God is not simply a nice theory. It is a
powerful truth that is palpable and transformative. You aren't
intended to simply read about God's love or acknowledge
that it exists. You are meant to experience it in every area
of your life. As his love transforms you, practice sharing
what you've learned with others. Don't overcomplicate it or
second-guess yourself. Simply give credit where it is due.
Use your words to praise the Lord because he has done great
things for you.

*God, your love is better than life. I hunger to know the power
of your love in palpable and practical ways today. I praise you
for what you are doing and what you will do!*

DECIDED

God also bound himself with an oath, so that those who received the promise could be perfectly sure that he would never change his mind.

HEBREWS 6:17 NLT

God will be faithful to his promises. He cannot and will not do anything that is against his Word. He is steadfast and unchanging in his love for his people. There is nothing that we can do to change his eternal plan. His power is greater than we understand, and his devotion to his people is unwavering. The covenant that he made cannot be broken, added to, or taken from.

God has already made up his mind about you. There is nothing you can do to change his perspective. He won't learn more about you and decide you aren't worth his devotion. He is committed to you for all of eternity. You cannot wander far enough away that he will lose sight of you. As his child, you will always have a place at his table. The security that you can find in his promises cannot be matched anywhere else.

Faithful One, thank you for your incredible patience. I'm so glad that you do not change your mind. I can always count on you.

KINDNESS OF GOD

When the kindness of God our Savior and His love for mankind appeared, He saved us, not on the basis of deeds which we did in righteousness, but in accordance with His mercy, by the washing of regeneration and renewing by the Holy Spirit.

TITUS 3:4-5 NASB

The kindness of God is not based on us. If his kindness were subject to our fickle behavior and selfishness, we would have every reason to despair. By nature, we are not dependable, steady, or unchanging. Rather, we are easily distracted, prone to wander, and easily persuaded to follow our selfish desires. Thankfully, we have the great privilege of putting our trust in our gracious Father. Every good gift he lavishes on us exemplifies the fact that he is eternally merciful and kind.

Don't be ashamed of your own tendency to be fickle or flighty. God knows everything about you. He knows all of your weaknesses and shortcomings. They aren't a surprise to him, and he isn't annoyed by them. Instead of being discouraged by your flaws, remember that they are an opportunity for his strength to be magnified.

Savior, help me remember that your kindness isn't dependent on my own actions. Help me feel secure in your love.

His Shelter

In the day of trouble,
he will treasure me in his shelter,
under the cover of his tent.
He will lift me high upon a rock,
out of reach from all my enemies
who surround me.

PSALM 27:5 TPT

Our difficult circumstances are not a reflection of God's thoughts about us. When we go through painful trials it is not because God is angry. Life is difficult for everyone. Each person's challenges look different, and we can't necessarily attribute them to God's favor or lack thereof. Instead of focusing on why something is happening we can focus on our reaction to difficult situations.

When you are in trouble, you can hide in the loving arms of your God and Savior. Run to your heavenly Father and let him shelter you. He will give you peace instead of worry. He will settle your heart and mind with his love. Don't let your troubles keep you from him. Be quick to ask him for help and trust that he is on your side.

Dear God, when I am going through hard times, I need your comforting presence and empowering strength. I will not stay away from you when I need you most!

Mindful of Mercy

Let not mercy and truth forsake you;
Bind them around your neck,
Write them on the tablet of your heart.

PROVERBS 3:3 NKJV

To bind mercy around our neck indicates that we must deliberately carry it around. In all we do, we should be aware of God's great mercy. With mercy directing our steps we will walk with humility, patience, and kindness. We will be ever aware that we have received a great gift we do not deserve. With mercy on our minds, we will be safe from pride, envy, and greed.

God's great mercy tells you exactly how he feels about you and how you should treat others. Through understanding mercy, you will see that God loves you, cares for you, and has gone to great lengths to save you. When those things are constantly on your mind, they will impact the way you view yourself and the way you love others. You can't be mindful of mercy and maintain selfishness, pride, bitterness, or anger. Bind mercy around your neck and let it transform you.

God, help me embrace mercy. Reveal to me how your mercy has impacted my life. As I gain understanding, help me love others as you've loved me.

No One Better

"Lord, God of Israel, there is no god like you in heaven
or on earth. You keep your agreement of love with your
servants who truly follow you."

2 Chronicles 6:14 ncv

We may have many ideas about who God is, but he is
bigger than all our thoughts. He alone is profoundly good,
kind, and just. No one can compare to his perfection, and no
one can claim to be as wise as he is. We could spend all our
days searching to find out more about him, but it would not
be enough time. Truly, no one compares to our God!

If you cringe when you think about an aspect of God,
you may need a perspective shift. Don't be ashamed if you
realize you're thinking wrongly. We all tend to see things in
a particularly biased way. Ask the Holy Spirit to help you see
God rightly. He will open your eyes and lead you to the truth.
He will give you grace to understand Scripture and will point
you to Jesus who is a perfect reflection of the Father.

*Lord God, I want to know you more. I don't want to put you
in a box or place my own limitations upon you. Show me how
wonderful you truly are.*

Glorious Grace

Thanks be to God for his indescribable gift!

2 CORINTHIANS 9:15 CSB

Grace cannot be earned or manipulated. It is not something available to some but withheld from others. It is the glorious gift of God offered freely to all who choose to receive it! It is given generously and abundantly. We may be tempted to put parameters on God's grace in an attempt to define it, but our own limited understanding doesn't change God's perfect gift.

The presence of God's grace in your life means you can have a fresh start whenever you want. It means that you aren't bound to sin or stuck under the weight of your mistakes. You can rely on what Christ did on the cross and trust that God has redeemed you. With this gift freely available to you remember that you will never graduate beyond the need for it. Humbly accept your constant and unchanging need for grace.

Gracious Jesus, thank you for removing the weight of our sin and shame. You are my liberator and my Savior. I can't thank you enough for the power of your grace!

Rock of Refuge

The LORD is my rock, my fortress and my deliverer;
my God is my rock, in whom I take refuge,
my shield and the horn of my salvation, my stronghold.

PSALM 18:2 NIV

The Lord is steady, and he will not be moved. Though natural disasters and conflicts may shake everything around us, God is unflinching. We remain sure-footed on the foundation of his love. He is our Rock, our fortress, and our deliverer. We can take refuge in him whenever we need it, for his door is always open. He always knows just what to say and do.

When troubles come, don't hesitate to run to God. He will not turn you away or shame you for asking for help. He is delighted when you turn to him. He loves it when you ask him for help. He is not impatient, short-tempered, or annoyed. You can go to him with confidence knowing that he will joyfully protect you and give you what you need.

Deliverer, I rely on you to save me and protect me. I trust you more than any other. Thank you for being steady and secure at all times.

God's Plan Prevails

Consider the work of God:
who can make straight what he has made crooked?

ECCLESIASTES 7:13 ESV

What God does, he does perfectly. No one can undo whatever God sets in motion. No one can thwart his plans or change the outcome. We can't see every detail of how he works, but we can trust that his mercy will always prevail! Our lack of understanding doesn't impact God's faithfulness. His promises are unbreakable, and he always keeps his word.

You can confidently yield control of your life to God. You don't have to hesitate or wonder if he is capable. His character has been proven by his faithfulness. You can trust that he will do what he says. There is great freedom found in surrendering to the One who created everything. Your admittance that you cannot control your life shows wisdom and an understanding of who God is. Your greatest strength will be found in embracing your weakness and trusting that God's ways are always higher than yours.

Mighty God, I sometimes struggle to trust you. I want to have control and I want to see each detail of my life perfectly. Instead, help me surrender to you and rest in your love.

GROUNDED IN TRUST

Enjoy prosperity while you can,
but when hard times strike,
realize that both come from God.
Remember that nothing is certain in this life.

ECCLESIASTES 7:14 NLT

Nothing in life is static. Change happens every day in big and little ways. We can't anticipate all the trials we will experience or witness in this lifetime. It is important to remember that no matter what season we find ourselves in, God remains steadfast, loving, and true. His character does not change based on our circumstances. In seasons of rejoicing God is good. In seasons of suffering God is still good.

When unexpected problems arise, you can ground yourself in truth. God is great no matter what is going on in your life. Turn your thoughts to his unfailing love. He will meet you wherever you are and will faithfully keep you steady. If you crave consistency and control, remember that God himself is the certainty you long for.

Lord, you are constant through life's shifting seasons. You are the same in suffering and rejoicing. Help me stand upon the unwavering foundation of your love.

Securely Attached

Keep yourselves in the love of God, looking forward to the mercy of our Lord Jesus Christ to eternal life.

JUDE 1:21 NASB

In faithful relationships there is a sense of safety, stability, and satisfaction. There is no reason to fear abandonment. Each person experiences feelings of acceptance and belonging. When we keep ourselves in the love of God, we are in the most secure relationship we can ever have. From this place we learn, grow, and transform.

What does it look like to keep yourself in the love of God? You can practice spending time in his presence. You can read Scripture and let it take root in your heart. You can praise him and ask for help when you need it. You can talk about his goodness with others, and you can develop the habit of welcoming him into every aspect of your life. There is no end to the goodness you can know through both hardships and blessings as you continually anchor yourself to the love of God.

Lord Jesus, thank you for the power of your love. It has transformed my life, and I am forever grateful. Help me remain rooted in your love all the days of my life!

MANY TITLES

Yahweh is my best friend and my shepherd.
I always have more than enough.

PSALM 23:1 TPT

We tend to see God with our own biases and preferences. We view him in light of our experiences and how we see the world. Some of us might lean toward perceiving him as Father, while others might be more comfortable with Friend, or King. No matter what we lean toward, it's important to remember that God embodies each of his titles. One title is not more accurate than the other. He is a perfect father, king, friend, shepherd, counselor, warrior, and advocate.

Today, ask God to reveal himself to you in a new way. There are always aspects of his personality to explore and discover. There are not enough days in your lifetime to develop an exhaustive experience of who God is. Try relating to him in a way that has been difficult for you in the past. Open your heart and let him heal your hurts or misconceptions. When you ask him for renewal, he will always be gentle and kind.

God, I want to know every part of you. Soften my heart and help me see you rightly. I don't want my biases to get in the way of experiencing all the goodness you offer. Heal my hurts and give me a fresh perspective.

Power of God

We have this treasure in earthen vessels, that the excellence
of the power may be of God and not of us.

2 Corinthians 4:7 nkjv

God loves to help us. He is not put off by our troubles or
our weaknesses. He knows how frail we are. He understands
that we have both strengths and weaknesses. None of this
intimidates or disgusts him. Though we may be our own
harshest critics, God sees us clearly and is our greatest
encourager. Our limitations should not keep us from God. It
doesn't matter how many times we fail or how ill-equipped
we think we are. He is powerful, and he is overflowing with
love for us.

Your weaknesses are simply an opportunity for God's
power to be seen more clearly. Where you are vulnerable,
he is strong. God's light shines brightly through the broken
areas of your life. You can give up the need to be perfect,
and rest in the truth that you are empowered, not limited, by
your weaknesses. Surrender to God's perfection and let your
striving cease.

*Faithful God, thank you for your constant encouragement.
Help me today; I need your strength. Be glorified in my life
and help me trust you with my weaknesses.*

Belonging to Him

The earth belongs to the LORD, and everything in it—
the world and all its people.

PSALM 24:1 NCV

If all the earth's people belong to the Lord, then no one is on the outside of his love. There isn't a single person who doesn't have the ability to be welcomed into his eternal family. We all have an equal opportunity to turn from our sins and accept the grace God offers. His desire is that we would all know him and experience the freedom for which we were intended.

Jesus paved the path to the Father so you can go to him freely and boldly. You can choose to deny God's presence in your life, but your heart's deepest longings will only be fulfilled by him. You were created for fellowship with your Maker. You belong to him and with him. When you engage in communion with him, you allow yourself to live fully and freely.

My Creator, I belong to you not only because you made me, but because I have surrendered my life to you. Refresh my spirit and give me eyes to see others as your beloved children as well.

HE'LL PROVIDE

God will supply all your needs according to his riches in glory in Christ Jesus.

PHILIPPIANS 4:19 CSB

God always welcomes his children into his presence with peace, love, and joy. He will not turn us away. When we pray it's important to remember that his resources are not limited. He is capable of meeting all our needs. We don't have to be sheepish or embarrassed by what we ask for. He does not give begrudgingly or with restraint. His timing and provision are perfect.

What do you need today? Is it encouragement, hope, or peace? Perhaps you need financial help or a wise counselor to advise you in an area where you feel stuck. Maybe you need a place to rest or compassion from someone you have disappointed. Whatever you need, God is able to provide for you. He is consistently generous and kind.

Faithful Provider, I trust you to meet my needs. You are such a good father and a faithful friend. I have known your provision before, and I trust that you will continue to help me. Thank you for your generosity.

IMMEASURABLE

To him who is able to do immeasurably more than all we ask
or imagine, according to his power that is at work within us,
to him be glory in the church and in Christ Jesus throughout
all generations.

EPHESIANS 3:20-21 NIV

The kingdom of God doesn't experience famine. It
doesn't have supply chain issues, nor does it have a shortage
of resources. In God's kingdom there is always abundance.
He is able to do immeasurably more than we can imagine.
Our prayers don't need to be minimal or modest. It is to our
benefit that we let go of small ideas and let him meet us with
his mercy and power.

You can't anticipate the details of the future, but you
can trust the One who sees everything clearly. From the
beginning to the end of your life, God knows exactly what
each day looks like. He knows how to fit the puzzle pieces
together perfectly. He is capable of equipping you with
everything you might need along the way. Trust in his
provision and you will not be left wanting.

*God, I trust in your provision. You know exactly what I need at
any given moment, and you will be faithful to provide it. Help
me not to limit your ability but to believe in your strength.*

THREE IN ONE

In the beginning was the Word,
and the Word was with God,
and the Word was God.

JOHN 1:1 ESV

We serve a God who is three in one. Each part is different from the other, but they are perfectly unified. Father, Son, and Spirit were together at the beginning. The three members of the Trinity have always existed in perfect harmony. They were together from before the birth of creation, and they will stay that way throughout eternity.

The idea of having one God who exists in three persons can be difficult to grasp. Instead of letting it cause confusion or mental frustration, marvel at the Lord's complexity. Ask him to teach you according to his Word. Dive into Scripture and ask difficult questions. Instead of ignoring certain parts of theology, be led by curiosity. Trust that God is capable of revealing the truth. Ask him for wisdom, and he will give it to you.

God, teach me about your complexities. I marvel at who you are, and I stand in awe of all you've done. Help me understand how the Trinity is perfectly woven together.

Take Notice

Everyone was gripped with great wonder and awe,
and they praised God, exclaiming,
"We have seen amazing things today!"

Luke 5:26 nlt

When Jesus healed the paralytic man everyone who witnessed it was awestruck. They recognized the miracle, and they responded by praising God. This is a simple but profound formula for what it means to follow Jesus. We often complicate Christianity, but it can be boiled down to observing the way God chooses to move, recognizing his power, and pausing to give him praise.

If you pay attention, you will see God moving in every area of your life. He is constantly sustaining you and faithfully providing for you. Take the time to notice what he is doing and praise him for it. As you develop this habit you will surely grow in love and affection for your Creator. The more you take note of his faithfulness, the more you will trust him for future provision.

God, help me see your faithfulness in my life. Thank you for your constant provision. I want to have eyes to see all that you are doing. I stand in awe of who you are.

Reasons to Rejoice

May all who seek You rejoice and be glad in You;
And may those who love Your salvation say continually,
"May God be exalted!"

PSALM 70:4 NASB

Gratitude can lead us straight into the presence of God. When we look for reasons to be thankful, it will open our eyes to the evidence of his goodness. When we take note of his goodness, we will begin to notice just how faithful he is. When we notice his faithfulness, we can't help but praise him for all he does. We can't truly love creation without acknowledging the Creator.

Today, look for reasons to rejoice. You have so much to be thankful for! How have you experienced God's goodness? Consider your relationships, the things that bring you delight, and the little pleasures of your day. Nothing is insignificant! Count the reasons and let it draw you toward God in praise. Rejoice in the way that he has provided for you.

Glorious One, I see so many reasons to praise you. There is so much to be thankful for. Open my eyes to see the ways you have been faithful to me.

HEART RESPONSE

I heard your voice in my heart say,
"Come, seek my face;"
my inner being responded,
"Yahweh, I'm seeking your face with all my heart."

PSALM 27:8 TPT

God invites us to look for him. He promises that when we look for him, we will find him. When we seek God, we respond to the invitation issued to each person from the beginning until the end of time. No matter how passionately we pursue God, let's not forget that he first pursued us! His love for us is what paved the way for us to be able to seek him at all.

God desires that you would find him. This isn't meant to be an overwhelming task or one more thing that you aren't accomplishing. He wants you close to him because he knows that his presence is where you will find true freedom. In his presence is where you find true joy, belonging, and satisfaction. He promises that if you look for him, you will find him.

God, I want to know you more. I want to experience the power of your love in new ways. Thank you for always being available to me.

Full Confidence

What then shall we say to these things?
If God is for us, who can be against us?

ROMANS 8:31 NKJV

God is faithful to his Word. What he promises, he faithfully fulfills. He is not a liar or a fake. He doesn't change his mind about us. His loyal love is never-ending, and his faithfulness knows no bounds. Even when we experience great suffering or darkness, God is still with us. He leads us through every valley, and we can trust his goodness every step of the way.

If you have surrendered your life to God, you are his child, and he will faithfully care for you. You are his and he will not forsake you. Your position in his family cannot be taken from you. You can have full confidence that you have a seat at the table. As an heir to his kingdom, you have full access to the protection that comes from being royal. God is for you; you have nothing to fear.

God, thank you for the power of your love which cannot be stolen or taken away. Help me trust you wholeheartedly. I have nothing to fear with you on my side.

April

The meek shall inherit the land
and delight themselves
in abundant peace.

PSALM 37:11 ESV

Saving Grace

That is the way we should live,
because God's grace that can save everyone has come.

TITUS 2:11 NCV

God's grace empowers us to live in alignment with his wisdom. Scripture instructs us that grace allows us to serve God rightly. Empowered by God's strength, we can live the way he intends us to. Our actions stem from the undeserved mercy that is so generously given to us.

The saving grace of Christ allows you to live in freedom from sin. Grace must be the foundation. Without it, you are bound to sin and trapped in legalism. You cannot work for extra grace. It is crucial to understand that you are no more or less deserving than anyone else. God's grace is given freely and without bias to everyone. Today, rejoice in the glorious gift that is yours for the taking.

God, thank you for the gift of grace. May it be the foundation for all that I do. I want to honor you with my actions because of what you've done for me.

RENEWED PERSPECTIVE

Do not be conformed to this age, but be transformed by the
renewing of your mind, so that you may discern what is the
good, pleasing, and perfect will of God.

ROMANS 12:2 CSB

Every day is a fresh opportunity to renew our
perspective. The truth of God has the power to transform
our minds continuously. We do not come to know the Lord
and instantaneously know what is right in every situation.
Our need for guidance and the wisdom of the Word doesn't
ever diminish. By consistently admitting our weaknesses
and walking with humility we leave space for the constant
renewing of our minds as God leads.

If you want your life to glorify God, you must first admit
your need for him. This need never changes or goes away.
Each day, each moment, you need his help and guidance.
Being transformed into his likeness is not a one-time
occurrence. The living Word transforms you throughout
your lifetime. Each person is on a journey with specific
needs and unique trajectories, but God's love remains the
same powerful source for everyone.

*Holy Spirit, continue to transform my mind. I want to be
able to discern God's will. Help me accept your guidance with
humility.*

Never Abandoned

The LORD will vindicate me;
your love, LORD, endures forever—
do not abandon the works of your hands.

PSALM 138:8 NIV

God does not forget his promises, and he does not abandon the works of his hands. We can rest in the loving care of our faithful Father. He will never stop working in our lives. He is constantly aware of us, and he is always moving on our behalf. He will never forsake those who seek him. Rather, he fights for us and surrounds us with his love.

God is acutely aware of you. He sees every minute detail of your life. He goes before you, and he hems you in. You have nothing to fear because the Lord your God is your savior and your vindication. You are fully secure and consistently cared for. Every anxiety, intrusive thought, or stress in your life is fully accounted for by God. He knows exactly what you need and precisely how to help you.

Lord, I rest in your faithfulness. Help me remember that you will never abandon me. I trust that you are moving in my life. Thank you for your enduring love.

HIS PURPOSE STANDS

Many are the plans in the mind of a man,
but it is the purpose of the LORD that will stand.

PROVERBS 19:21 ESV

No matter how much control we think we have over our lives, God is the one with true authority. This isn't to say we can't make plans, but it's important to remember the only thing that will truly last forever is the purpose of the Lord. There is nothing that we can manufacture or accomplish that will outlast what God has done.

When you hold your plans loosely, trusting God's will over your own, you set yourself up for success. Disappointment over changes or failures isn't as poignant when your highest goal is to honor the Lord. As you trust in him, he will give you confidence that cannot be shaken by changing circumstances or unmet expectations. He remains steadfast and strong whether or not life looks the way you think it should.

Lord, I'm so glad that you aren't surprised by the things that throw me off. You are my confidence, and I trust you to lead me through every twist and turn of this life.

Seasons and Cycles

For everything there is a season,
a time for every activity under heaven.

ECCLESIASTES 3:1 NLT

When we see our circumstances as a gauge of God's favor, hard times can cause us to question his goodness. Our faith is shaken easily when our foundation isn't strong. Our confidence is meant to be rooted in the only thing that never changes instead of being dependent on circumstances. God's character is consistent. While we are subject to the seasons of life, God is constant and steady at all times.

Do you feel like you are on shaky ground, being tossed around by ever-changing circumstances? If your answer is yes, perhaps you've put your hope in what's happening around you instead of the consistency of the Lord. Ask God to strengthen your resolve and keep you steady even though the seasons of life can be unpredictable. Even when you are blindsided by unexpected change, you can lean on the Lord, who is reliable and unwavering.

Father, help me trust you no matter what season of life I'm in. I want to trust in you more than my circumstances. You are worthy of my praise and devotion despite what's happening around me.

PICKED FIRST

In Him we also have obtained an inheritance, having been predestined according to the purpose of Him who works all things in accordance with the plan of His will.

EPHESIANS 1:11 NASB

In Christ, we share in the inheritance of God's kingdom. We haven't gained this position by luck or happenstance. God chose us before we could even think of choosing him. He predestined his children to spend eternity with him. Our glorious inheritance comes from his hands alone. He has invited each of us to share in the riches of his glory because he delights in his creation.

Have you ever waited to be chosen for something and then worried that you wouldn't make the cut? You don't have to worry about this with the Lord. If you desire to know him, you can be sure that he has already chosen you. He loves you more than you know. He delights in you, and there is no need to second-guess his decision to choose you. Let him love you and enjoy the full life that he intends for you.

Lord, thank you for choosing me as your own. I want to bloom in the light of your love! I choose you, God, because you first chose me.

Grace First

Whether you eat or drink, live your life
in a way that glorifies and honors God.

1 Corinthians 10:31 tpt

Our desire to glorify God comes from an understanding
of what he has already done for us. We seek to live in a
way that pleases him because we are so thankful for his
redemption and mercy. We know that our good works
do not gain us salvation, but we live in a way that honors
Christ's sacrifice. We are not bound to a list of rules, but we
acknowledge that God knows what is best for our lives. His
ways are higher than ours. We can trust that if God declares
something as good, it must be so.

When your obedience to God is founded in undeserved
grace, your service to him will be joyous and without
obligation. If you feel like you are constantly striving to
follow the right rules, it may be time to evaluate your
understanding of grace. Scripture is clear that the law is
summed up by loving God and loving others. If these two
things are your focus, your life will glorify God.

Lord, I want to worship you with my words and actions.
Help me honor Christ's sacrifice in all I do. Thank you for the
undeserved grace you have shown me.

Set Apart

"Before I formed you in the womb I knew you;
Before you were born I sanctified you;
I ordained you a prophet to the nations."

JEREMIAH 1:5 NKJV

The Father of creation set each of us apart from the beginning and called us his own. He has a purpose and a divine destiny for each of us. Some may travel the world or speak in front of crowds of people. Some may faithfully tend to their home or work in the same office for 20 years. The details of our lives aren't nearly as important as the foundation they are built on.

Being set apart by God doesn't fit into one easy to define formula. Whether your life is simple or extravagant by human terms, the important part is that you know him, love him, and follow him. If your ways are committed to God, he will make your path straight and help you to honor him. Your path might look different from those around you but that doesn't make it more or less valuable.

Lord, thank you for calling me with a specific purpose. Help me love you and others while living with integrity. I want to honor you with every detail of my life.

WANTED

"You are worthy, our Lord and God,
to receive glory and honor and power,
because you made all things.
Everything existed and was made,
because you wanted it."

REVELATION 4:11 NCV

At the core of each person is a deep need for belonging and purpose. We all want to be accepted, loved, and wanted. We remain empty-handed when we seek to satisfy those things on our own. Truly, our search must begin and end in the presence of God. He created us, and we are meant to experience the fullness of life through him.

God created the world for his good pleasure. There is no need to wonder if you are wanted or desired. The God of the universe knit you together, and he created you intentionally. You were made with purpose and pleasure. Your very being brings delight to your heavenly Father. As you spend time in his presence today, ask him to speak to your heart about the deep love he has for you.

Father God, you are worthy of all the praise, adoration, and trust I can give you. You loved me first, and you love me best. Fill my life with hope and confidence today!

Look to Jesus

"I can do nothing on my own. I judge only as I hear, and my judgment is just, because I do not seek my own will, but the will of him who sent me."

JOHN 5:30 CSB

Jesus himself didn't rely on his own perspective, strength, or knowledge. He was fully dependent on the Father. If Jesus, in all of his perfection, understood the need for constant connection with God, why do we feel so adamant about our own independence? Instead of insisting that we can navigate life on our own, we should look to Jesus' example of partnering with God in everything we do.

It is good to develop friendship and fellowship with God. You can stay close to him by reading the Scriptures, praying, and practicing his ways. Jesus looked to his Father every day, and you can do the same. Turn your attention toward him and practice including him in each part of your day. The more you invite the Father into your rhythms, the more natural it will become.

Lord, I don't want to act like I know better than you. I humble my heart before you and admit my need for you. Help me depend on you consistently throughout my day.

ABUNDANT LIFE

"The thief comes only to steal and kill and destroy;
I have come that they may have life,
and have it to the full."

JOHN 10:10 NIV

God's desire is for us to experience abundant life. Every good gift comes from him. He is the author of our salvation and the provider of all our needs. Pain and conflict do not come from him. He is fully capable of using hardship to our benefit, but his original intention is not for us to suffer. As we navigate this life, it's important to remember that perfection is coming. One day we will live in God's presence and experience the true fullness of life for which we were intended.

If you feel resentment building in your heart, ask God for help. He can soften your heart and remind you that he desires good things for you. The trials in your life are not his doing. Ask him for clarity and the wisdom to navigate what you are facing. He is kind and faithful. He sees you with loving eyes and desires to give you mercy.

God, I trust in your goodness. Help me see your faithfulness in my life. Equip me to handle hardship and give me endurance to be faithful until you return.

Power of Confession

If we confess our sins, he is faithful and just to forgive us our
sins and to cleanse us from all unrighteousness.

1 JOHN 1:9 ESV

When we have sinned, it doesn't do any good to resist
taking responsibility for our actions. It is much better to
confess and try to repair any damage done. A person of
integrity asks for forgiveness and seeks to change their
behavior. Secret sins and even obvious sins are fodder
for shame. There is so much power in confessing our
struggles and wrongdoings. When we readily admit to our
weaknesses, we give others the freedom to do the same.
Vulnerability begets vulnerability.

There is nothing you can confess that is too grievous
for God to forgive. Instead of carrying the shame of your
mistakes, give them readily to Him. He wants to forgive you.
He wants you to experience the freedom only he can offer. He
doesn't want you to punish yourself when Jesus has already
borne the weight of sin. Let yourself relax and trust that when
you confess, your sins are fully and completely forgiven.

*Savior, thank you for the power of your forgiveness which frees
me from guilt and shame. Help me confess quickly when I do
something wrong. I want to honor you in all that I do.*

Established Steps

We can make our plans,
but the LORD determines our steps.

PROVERBS 16:9 NLT

We all make plans in order to reach our goals. We evaluate the steps it will take to get from where we are to where we want to be. Unfortunately, even the best-laid plans will have unforeseen challenges. We cannot account for illness, loss, or economic change. No matter how many unexpected things happen, or how many times our plans are interrupted, we can trust in the steadiness of the Lord.

When your life is surrendered to God, he is the one who determines your steps. He will faithfully guide you as you keep your eyes on him. Even when the path doesn't look the way you expected, you can trust that he knows what is best. With every twist and turn you can remain steady and encouraged, knowing that God sees each of your days clearly.

Faithful Leader, I am so glad that you are not worried about the things that throw me off. Fill me with peace and help me trust you with all my heart.

All Things

I can do all things
through Him who strengthens me.

PHILIPPIANS 4:13 NASB

When Paul talks about being able to accomplish anything he is referencing the ability to be content no matter what his life looked like. Sometimes we use this scripture as an encouragement that we can achieve whatever we want as long as we trust God. While God does empower us to do wonderful things, he is far more concerned with the state of our heart. Being content with what we are given matters more than accomplishing our to do list.

Are you content with what God has given you? Even the idea of contentment is difficult to grasp in a culture that idolizes materialism and satisfying experiences. If you are constantly looking for the next measure of gratification it might be time to ask God to help you find contentment. Paul knew that the secret was acknowledging all that Jesus had done for him. Using his example, ask God to reveal areas of your life where you are sitting in dissatisfaction.

Faithful One, like Paul, I want to be content in every situation. You have provided for each of my needs so faithfully. Help me acknowledge my blessings each day and keep my eyes focused on you.

Expressions of Love

The Holy Spirit produces this kind of fruit in our lives:
love, joy, peace, patience, kindness, goodness,
faithfulness, gentleness, and self-control.
There is no law against these things!

Galatians 5:22-23 nlt

There is so much substance in the fruit of God's Spirit. If we focused on the various expressions of his love for weeks, we would barely scratch the surface. We will never reach the end of our pursuit. The Holy Spirit gives us revelations of God's goodness each new day. We are always learning and growing in the length, breadth, and depth of his love.

Choose one of the fruits of the Spirit to meditate on throughout the day. Look for ways to incorporate it into your interactions, your speech, and your choices. Make it your intention to move through your day sowing seeds of that fruit as much as possible. As you do, remember God's love for you is more than enough to supply whatever you need!

Holy Spirit, I want my life to be full of your fruit. Show me ways I can grow in your goodness as I incorporate your ways into my day.

WALK IN THE LIGHT

Then Jesus spoke to them again, saying, "I am the light of the
world. He who follows Me shall not walk in darkness,
but have the light of life."

JOHN 8:12 NKJV

Jesus invites us to walk with him in the light of his love.
He provides life-giving truth, wise counsel, and powerful
mercy to liberate and transform us. Why would we choose
to walk in a cloud of confusion when he offers us the fog-
clearing light of his fellowship? When we walk with him,
he shares his resources with us, strengthening our souls in
his love and pouring the goodness of his presence into our
hearts, minds, and lives.

You never need to fear the light of his presence. In his
presence there is no condemnation or shame. Nothing is
hidden, and you will be met with perfect love. God sees you
clearly, and he is not surprised by what you want to hide. He
offers you freedom and the soul rest that comes from laying
down your burdens. Today, rest in his presence and live in
his light.

*Light of the world, in you all things are made clear. You don't
leave any shadows. There is light, life, peace, joy, and so much
love in your presence. I choose to follow you!*

Filtered through Jesus

Trust the LORD with all your heart,
and don't depend on your own understanding.

PROVERBS 3:5 NCV

Our understanding is lacking, and we cannot depend on our own perceptions. In every situation there are things we cannot control, dynamics we cannot make sense of, and obstacles we cannot anticipate. When we insist on maintaining a false sense of control, we let pride get in the way of God's best for us. He knows our weaknesses, and he offers us the ability to lean on his infinite wisdom. We have access to unlimited knowledge and understanding. Even so, we often refuse his help both consciously and subconsciously.

Today, invite God to give you wisdom in an area you've been trying to handle on your own. It's easy to get so caught up in something that you simply forget to ask for help. Remember that he is eager and able to help you navigate every area of your life. You can lean on him for help in everything from the complicated relationship you have with a friend to the feelings of anxiety you get when you realize your schedule is too full. Trust him and let him lead you.

Lord Jesus, I trust you with all my heart. I depend on you, especially when nothing makes sense, and I cannot see a way forward. You always know just what to do!

Satisfying Truth

"I am the bread of life," Jesus told them. "No one who comes to me will ever be hungry, and no one who believes in me will ever be thirsty again."

JOHN 6:35 CSB

We've all eaten a meal and then been hungry a short time later. Though we filled our stomachs, our appetite was not quenched. We need to eat in order to live, and we can't expect one meal to last for our entire lifetime. Beyond physical nourishment, we need spiritual nourishment. Our soul needs to be fed by the life-giving presence of the Lord. Just like one meal won't keep us satiated physically, one encounter with God will not meet our soul's needs forever. We need consistent communion with him.

Jesus is the feast you never have to leave; he is the One who satisfies your soul at every level. When you feel deeply dissatisfied or as if you are missing something, run to Jesus. You will find a sense of belonging in his presence that cannot be matched anywhere else. Woven into your very being is the need for fellowship with your Creator. You cannot run from it, and you cannot satisfy it on your own. Go confidently to his presence and let your soul find true satisfaction.

Savior, in your presence, I find my strength. You are better than the finest feast.

Consider This

God chose the foolish things of the world to shame the wise;
God chose the weak things of the world to shame the strong.

1 Corinthians 1:27 niv

Most of us are very aware of our weaknesses. We know what we lack and how we fall short. If success in the kingdom of God was dependent on us overcoming our faults, we would be in a dire situation. Thankfully, God doesn't care about our insufficiencies. He can easily take a fool and make him wise. He can use the weakest areas of our lives and be glorified in them. God doesn't require you to change anything about yourself in order to be valued.

God covers you with the fullness of his mercy. He blesses you with his presence no matter how imperfect you are. He can be magnified in your life no matter how inadequate you think you are. In the areas where you see yourself as foolish, God sees as opportunities to reveal the wonders of his love. He doesn't waste anything, and he delights in astounding you with the power of his presence.

God, remind me who I am and how much you love me. Meet me with the power of your presence as I yield to your leadership. I trust you!

CREATED WITH PURPOSE

Who are you, a mere human being, to argue with God?
Should the thing that was created say to the one who
created it, "Why have you made me like this?"

ROMANS 9:20 NLT

Comparison is a trap that can lead us to envy others and
belittle ourselves. There will always be someone else who is
better at something than we are, but that doesn't make us any
less valuable. Each of us come with our own strengths and
weaknesses, and those are specific to the will of God and his
purposes. He is well aware of our flaws, and he still declares
his creation to be good. If the Maker does not despair over
our weaknesses, then neither should we.

God knew what he was doing when he created you.
He didn't make you like anyone else. You are unique, and
you were made to thrive in your created purpose. If you
are looking for what that is, consider your natural gifts. The
things that make your soul come alive and feel easy are likely
the things that God has gifted to you specifically. Embrace
the way he made you and continue to submit your strengths
and weaknesses to his purposes.

Lord, I don't want to get caught in the trap of comparison.
Help me honor the way you created me. Give me grace to
allow others to do the same.

Wait for It

Still the vision awaits its appointed time;
it hastens to the end—it will not lie.
If it seems slow, wait for it;
it will surely come; it will not delay.

Habakkuk 2:3 esv

In the space between promise and fulfillment, there lies an invitation to wait. Nothing is as black and white as it may seem. We make vows and then have to walk them out. What seems simple when we are young grows complex in the nuances of maturity and experience. Sometimes the answer isn't as easy as following a set of instructions. Sometimes the answer is time. We all must learn to wait in life; those who learn to wait well practice patience.

Patience is not easy, and you've probably experienced seasons of life that prove it. Hope is what makes waiting doable. When you believe the end is worth it, you can choose to persevere through the waiting. Even when the vision seems slow in coming, you are motivated by the promise of what's to come. Even when you desperately long for the perfection of eternity, you can persevere through the trials of life because you know that God will keep his promise.

Faithful God, your promises will not fail. Strengthen me in the in-between spaces. Give me patience to wait and help me trust in your faithfulness.

Eternal Perspective

Teach us to number our days,
That we may present to You a heart of wisdom.

PSALM 90:12 NASB

Life is fleeting. Since we are here for a limited time, we should live wisely and intentionally. It is good to evaluate our priorities in light of the age to come. Are we focused on things that will last, or are we consistently swayed by worldly satisfaction? Thoughts of eternity shouldn't cause us to feel frantic; rather, we should be soberly aware of how we spend our time, energy, and resources.

God has each of your days in his hands. He knows exactly how much time you will spend on earth. He isn't stressed by the length of your life, and you shouldn't be either. Keep your eyes on him, and he will direct your steps. Let him lead you. Ask for wisdom when you need it and trust that every moment of your life is under his watchful eye.

Everlasting One, I don't want to waste my life on meaningless things. I look to you for leadership and wisdom. Help me trust you with each of my days.

Pure Religion

True spirituality that is pure in the eyes of our Father God is to make a difference in the lives of the orphans, and widows in their troubles, and to refuse to be corrupted by the world's values.

JAMES 1:27 TPT

Genuine spirituality is not found in creeds or ideologies. It's easy to get caught up in maintaining a set of rules that we think will make us better. The truth is that what really matters is accepting God's grace and treating those around us with dignity and kindness. If we genuinely want to honor God with our lives, we must look at our hearts first.

Caring for the orphan and the widow might sound romantic but the reality is that it's often inconvenient and costly. It's much easier to conform to a set of rules than it is to dole out sacrificial love. Unfortunately, the rules you make for yourself only stand in the way of experiencing the abundant grace and mercy that God offers. God's love is meant to change you from the inside out; his delight in you motivates you to lay your life down for others.

God, you are rich in mercy and generous in grace. Help me look for opportunities to help those in need. I want to love others as you have loved me.

Evermore

Seek the LORD and His strength;
Seek His face evermore!

1 CHRONICLES 16:11 NKJV

Eternity is too much for us to grasp. In our finite lives, we only truly comprehend what we know here and now. The idea of seeking God's face forever doesn't fully compute. Despite our limited understanding, we anticipate and look forward to the day that we will dwell in his presence forever. We know, deep down, that we were made to be near to God.

No matter how far along you are in your relationship with God, there is so much you simply don't know. You could spend your entire life seeking him and it wouldn't be enough time. This is the beauty of eternity. You will live perfectly and wholly in his presence for more time than your mind can comprehend. There will be no end to your relationship with God. Let the promise of eternity with him motivate you to persevere through this life. As you catch glimpses of his glory may they fill you with hope for what is to come.

Glorious God, you have no beginning, and you have no end. It is hard to imagine, but I look forward to eternity with you. You are my strength, my hope, and my source!

Reason to Hope

I say to myself, "The Lord is mine,
so I hope in him."

LAMENTATIONS 3:24 NCV

We belong to God. He is our Father, and we are his beloved children. He withholds nothing good from those who follow him. He lovingly leads us, and is capable of handling every burden, question, and hope. We don't need to hold back anything from him! He isn't afraid of our big emotions or concerned about our doubts. He is nearby, and he has made himself ours through Christ.

What hope there is in fellowship with Christ! What relief there is in the conviction that he knows you, loves you, and redeems you. There isn't a part of you he rejects. Throw off the fear that hinders you from wholeheartedly bringing your life before the Lord and put your hope fully in his unfailing love!

Lord, I am yours, and you are mine. You are my help, my strength, and my solace. You are all I need and so much more! Everything I am, every part of me, I bring to you today. My whole hope is in you.

Embodied Peace

The peace of God, which surpasses all understanding,
will guard your hearts and minds in Christ Jesus.

PHILIPPIANS 4:7 CSB

The peace of God is meant to settle our minds. It passes all understanding, flooding our nervous systems with the regulating power of God's presence. It guards our hearts and minds providing protection from outside stress and our own emotions. Even when it would make sense to be overwhelmed or full of worry, we can trust that God will give us peace.

When you feel anxious and worried, God's peace is available to you. When you don't know how to navigate a situation, the peace of God is available to you. Take some time to invite him into whatever situation you are facing. No matter how serious or trivial, God wants to be involved in the everyday details of your life. Don't stubbornly insist on figuring things out alone. Partner with God and accept the abundant gift of peace he offers you.

Prince of Peace, wash over me today. Align my heart and mind with you. Help me lean on your peace and trust that your understanding is higher than mine.

He Will Do It

"From the east I summon a bird of prey;
from a far-off land, a man to fulfill my purpose.
What I have said, that I will bring about;
what I have planned, that I will do."

ISAIAH 46:11 NIV

God is dependable and trustworthy. He always does what he says. We may wonder how or when he will fulfill his promises, but we don't need to doubt it will happen. When we learn to take God at his Word, trusting him to faithfully follow through on his promises, we can walk through the uncertainty of this life with confidence. We can rest fully assured that his nature is unchanging, and he won't go back on his word. His promises are not contingent upon us.

If you struggle to trust in God's promises, take some time to write out all the ways he has been faithful in the past. As you take note of his goodness, you will be reassured of his ability to do what he says. The more you acknowledge this, the more you will develop the confident expectation that he will be faithful in the future. Look to the Word, your own experiences, and the experiences of those around you to see numerous accounts of God keeping his promises.

Promise Keeper, you are the God who does what he says he will do. Increase my faith and fill me with confidence.

Spirit of Truth

"When the Spirit of truth comes, he will guide you into all the truth, for he will not speak on his own authority, but whatever he hears he will speak, and he will declare to you the things that are to come."

JOHN 16:13 ESV

The Holy Spirit is a tremendous gift to us. The Spirit guides us into all truth by expanding our understanding of God and revealing his wonderful nature to us. Christ left his spirit as a gift after the resurrection. He knew that we would need constant help and guidance. He knew that we would need to be reassured and reminded of the truth. Without the presence of the Holy Spirit, we are prone to wander away from God.

The Holy Spirit is your teacher and counselor. He is the one who guides you into the presence of God. He is the one who stirs your heart to behave in a certain way. He is the one who reminds you to depend on God's promises when life is difficult. The Spirit within you testifies that you belong to God, and he gives you confidence that you are on the right path. Trust in his leadership and seek to follow him closely.

Holy Spirit, I want to be led by you. Thank you for pointing me to the Father. I would be lost without you. Help me follow you closely and lean on your understanding.

Way of Life

You will show me the way of life,
granting me the joy of your presence
and the pleasures of living with you forever.

PSALM 16:11 NLT

God is faithful to lead his children through life. As we follow him, he becomes our prize, our pleasure, and our portion. He is more than enough to satisfy the longings of our hearts. He is overwhelmingly good and consistently gracious. In his presence we find true joy, and we realize that communion with the Creator is what we were made for.

You were created to know God, not just in little moments but throughout every season of your life. Run into his courts with praise and follow him as he guides you on the path which he himself has laid out for you. It is a good path, planned for your good, and there is joy in his fellowship along the way. He will never leave you or forsake you. Don't deprive yourself of the goodness he has planned for you today.

Faithful One, thank you for leading me. Thank you for being close and available whenever I need you. I come to you with my heart wide open today, ready to receive all you have to offer.

EVERY CIRCUMSTANCE

May the Lord of peace Himself continually grant you peace
in every circumstance. The Lord be with you all!

2 THESSALONIANS 3:16 NASB

The Lord our God is peace. When he is with us, so is the
presence of peace. This means we have peace available to us
at all times and in all circumstances. No matter how difficult
we think a situation is, God sees it clearly and is able to
navigate it with ease. Peace comes from trusting that God is
both capable and willing to lovingly lead each of his children
through life.

Whatever you are facing today, the peace of God is
available to you. Lean into the nearness of God. Turn your
attention to him and invite him to bring his peace into your
situation. Trust him to do it, for he has never met a challenge
he couldn't overcome. Jesus slept peacefully through a
raging storm, and he offers you this same powerful peace to
carry you through your own storms. Lean on him, for he is
sufficient, and he is not overwhelmed!

*Lord Jesus, you are the Prince of Peace. Meet me with the
peace of your presence today. I don't want to walk through life
depending on my own abilities when I can surrender to you.*

MAY

My lips will glorify you
because your faithful love
is better than life.

PSALM 63:3 CSB

Friend To All

Do your best to live as everybody's friend.

ROMANS 12:18 TPT

Jesus was a friend to everyone. His kindness didn't change whether someone was young, old, rich, poor, healthy, or sick. If we want to follow his example, we must do the same. The way we treat others should not depend on our opinions of them or what we think they deserve. Instead, we are called to love the way Jesus did. He elevated those who society deemed unacceptable and unworthy. When we mirror his actions, we will be kind, accepting, and gracious to all people.

Do you prioritize kindness, or is the way you treat others based on your own opinions? Today, remember the undeserved grace you have received. Let God's favor in your own life motivate you to be gentle and gracious toward others. Ask God to help you love others the way he has loved you. As you seek to have his perspective, he will soften your heart and teach you how to be merciful and kind in every situation.

Lord, help me be kind even when it is difficult. I want to be at peace with the people in my life. Help me promote peace and discourage disunity. You are the best example to follow!

Good Gifts

Mercy and truth have met together;
Righteousness and peace have kissed.
Truth shall spring out of the earth,
And righteousness shall look down from heaven.

PSALM 85:10-11 NKJV

God's presence is available to all his beloved children.
We yield our hearts to him, and he meets us with unending
mercy. He showers us with good gifts, and he provides for all
our needs. He does not withhold his goodness, and he does
not stay hidden when we seek him. When we follow him,
surely our lives will be filled with goodness.

If you are in Christ, you can be sure of God's mercy for
you today. There is no question of his love! His redemptive
power can restore your hope and rejuvenate your heart. He
wants you to enjoy the goodness of his presence. In him you
will find mercy, truth, righteousness, and peace. If you reach
out, he will meet you wherever you are.

*Merciful God, I need your power to refresh my heart. I am
desperate for your restorative touch. You have good things in
store for me, and I trust that you will keep your promises.*

Hold on to Hope

Let us hold firmly to the hope that we have confessed,
because we can trust God to do what he promised.

HEBREWS 10:23 NCV

God's faithfulness is based on his character alone. It isn't
dependent on our ability to perform or follow through. We
don't need to strive for perfection in order for God to keep
his promises. Through Christ's death on the cross, every
requirement for holiness has been met. We get to experience
all the benefits of God's mercy without shouldering the cost.

When you find yourself in difficult situations, you can
firmly plant your trust in the One who is faithful. When you
choose to hope instead of despair, your heart fills with the
peace of God rather than the agony of doubt. Though you
cannot forecast every outcome, you can trust the One who
sees the end from the beginning. His love never fails, not even
when you are disappointed or discouraged. Hope keeps you
connected to the restorer who is always faithful to his word!

*Faithful One, I hold firmly to the hope that you will do what
you say. I don't have to manage or control anything when it
comes to your promises. Keep my heart at peace as I continue
to surrender to you.*

ALL WE REQUIRE

His divine power has given us everything required for life
and godliness through the knowledge of him who called us
by his own glory and goodness.

2 PETER 1:3 CSB

We are constantly confronted with what we lack in this
life. In our consumerist society someone is always selling
something that is better, faster, or easier so we might tend to
reach for the new thing to fix us. It is hard to settle into what
is already ours and to realize that what we have is enough for
the moment.

God's power is present with us through his Spirit.
Everything that is required of us is offered through the
grace of his fellowship. Instead of getting burdened by the
overwhelming demand always in front of us, we gain clarity
and strength in knowing what the goodness of God actually
entails. All we really need today for life and godliness is
available to us. Thank God for that!

Lord, help me be grounded in your present mercy. Give me
clarity for what I actually need in order to put my attention and
energy in the right places today. Thank you for all you provide.
I need to be aware of your provision each and every day.

Wonderful Things

Lord, you are my God;
I will exalt you and praise your name,
for in perfect faithfulness
you have done wonderful things,
things planned long ago.

Isaiah 25:1 niv

Scripture displays a rich history of God's faithful love helping people through the depths of their trials. He consistently led his people into life-giving restoration, hope, and joy. Whether we read the Word or hear the testimonies of other believers, we can strengthen our resolve and grow in hope by learning how God faithfully moved in the hearts and lives of others.

Surely, God has sustained you and those around you. Ask other believers to share what he has done in their lives. Be encouraged by the specific and unique ways he has shown up. Take note of how he's been faithful in your own life. Let this collection of testimonies strengthen your faith and give you a greater assurance of God's ability to do what he says. The God who did wonderful things long ago still does wonderful things.

God, I want to trust your faithful love in deeper ways. Give me greater assurance of your mercy and kindness.

Sustained

I lay down and slept;
I woke again, for the LORD sustained me.
I will not be afraid of many thousands of people
who have set themselves against me all around.

PSALM 3:5-6 ESV

In musical terms, when a note is sustained its sound rings steadily over a period of time. If a note on the keyboard is held with the sustain pedal pressed, the sound continues until the key is released. Similarly, God sustains us. It is not difficult for him. His love is the ongoing tone that rings in the background of our lives. It never diminishes as it melds with the sounds of our everyday life.

When you lay down to sleep and when you awaken each morning, the Lord is the one who sustains your life. There's no reason to fear what each day will bring, for the love of God rings strong and true, never ending or changing. When everything around you feels unpredictable and unmanageable trust in the consistency of God. Your circumstances are unreliable, but God's love is steady and will sustain you for all your days.

Lord, thank you for your power which sustains me. I will not fear anything today, for you are with me. I will trust in your unchanging love.

Seek and Find

"If you look for me wholeheartedly, you will find me."

JEREMIAH 29:13 NLT

God does not hide in places where it is difficult to discover him. If we have eyes to see, we will find him just as certainly as the sunlight eventually filters through the clouds. He will not abandon us when we need him. God is faithful to show up in perfect timing. When we open our eyes to see the work of his hands, we will notice his fingerprints everywhere.

Have you ever been surprised to find God in a place that was unexpected? Jesus shocked the religious people of his day by dining with people labeled as sinners. He talked to women who weren't his family, he touched people with leprosy, and he taught about God to multitudes in places other than the temple. Look for God wholeheartedly, and you will find him. His presence in your life may look different than you expect but it will not be absent. It's not a question of if, but when and where he will meet you!

Lord God, I'm so grateful that you are not bound by the laws and expectations of humanity. You are bigger, better, and kinder than I can understand. Help me see you even in unexpected places.

True Love

God's Word is something to sing about!
He is true to his promises, his word can be trusted,
and everything he does is reliable and right.

PSALM 33:4 TPT

There is a plethora of love songs out in the world.
Though the subject seems to have been exhausted, our
hunger for them has not. We love to express our longings
in poetry, art, and song. We never tire of love stories! There
are, in much the same way, many expressions of God's
love recorded in the Bible. There is no earthly love story
that compares to what God has done for his people. The
belonging and acceptance we all long for is found in the
presence of our Maker.

God is true to his promises. Everything he does is laced
with loving-kindness. He restores strained relationships
and replenishes weary hearts. He is wise and just, faithful,
and true. How has God's love impacted your life? Take time
today to dwell on what he has done for you. You are free to
gush about God's goodness because it cannot be exaggerated.
His love for you is better than anything else you will ever
experience.

*God, your love is better than life. You have been so good to
me, and I won't stop singing your praises. I love you!*

Unchanging

"I, the LORD, do not change; therefore you,
the sons of Jacob, have not come to an end."

MALACHI 3:6 NASB

We would be in trouble if the Lord changed his mind about us. If he gave up on his love, what could we possibly rely on? We would be lost and without hope. We would be overcome and overwhelmed. The good news is that there's no need to dwell on impossible situations. The Lord does not change. He is the same yesterday, today, and forever. His character is steady, and his love toward us is unending.

Does your life reflect the knowledge that God is constant and secure? There is no stress or anxiety that is too big for him. There is no trial that he cannot handle, and there is no situation that he cannot foresee. Today, ask the Holy Spirit for a fresh revelation of God's unchanging nature. Let his steadiness give you confidence and a sense of safety that overflows into every part of your life.

Faithful Lord, I'm so grateful for your unchanging nature. Where I have misunderstood you, please open up my eyes. Allow me to see you rightly.

Continual Connection

Let this hope burst forth within you, releasing a
continual joy. Don't give up in a time of trouble,
but commune with God at all times.

ROMANS 12:12 TPT

Continual communion with God is an invitation he
offers each of us. He has the time, energy, and attention span
to hear us whenever we call on him. We will never get a busy
signal in place of his listening ear. His ability to pay close
attention to every aspect of his creation is beyond our own
understanding. He is always there when we need him no
matter how often that is.

There is such peace and joy found in God's presence.
Knowing he is accessible is both reassuring and empowering.
When you face troubles of many kinds, you can confidently
go to God. He will never turn you away or tell you he cannot
help. You can continually connect with him no matter the
time of day. Throw off your hindrances and excuses and take
him up on his glorious offer. Let your soul find rest and joy
in his presence.

*God, thank you for the continual communion I can have with
you. I don't want to ignore this generous gift. Keep me close,
and comfort me with your presence.*

Just Ask

"Until now you have not asked for anything in my name.
Ask and you will receive, so that your joy will be the fullest
possible joy."

JOHN 16:24 NCV

God is delighted when we come to him. He is a good
Father who is already well aware of our weaknesses. We are
not more virtuous or holy when we withhold our desires and
needs from him. We don't have to be strong or insist that we
are capable on our own. He is secure in love, and he wants us
to share our most vulnerable selves with him.

You may not be accustomed to recognizing your needs
or asking for help. You may have learned to use your own
resourcefulness early in life and therefore see neediness as
something to avoid. The truth is being human means that
you inevitably have weaknesses. This is not a bad thing. God
delights in you when you ask him for help. As you embrace
your neediness, you create room for God's strength to be
magnified.

*Lord, I don't want to withhold my requests because of my
own pride. I bring you my real needs, longings, and hopes. As
you take them into your hands, I trust that you are able to
care for me.*

NOT YET SEEN

Though you have not seen him, you love him; though not
seeing him now, you believe in him, and you rejoice with
inexpressible and glorious joy, because you are receiving the
goal of your faith, the salvation of your souls.

1 PETER 1:8-9 CSB

Even though we have not yet seen God face-to-face, we
know him through fellowship, prayer, and the Word. We see
his hand at work in our lives and we trust that he is faithfully
keeping his promises. We vow to follow him for all our days
and refuse to turn back. The journey we take with God is
not dependent on what we see but on what we know is true.
There is a great reward for those who believe in God and all
he does.

Your faith is delightful to God. He knows how difficult
it can be to trust in what you cannot see. Each step of faith
you take, no matter how small, brings great pleasure to
God. Don't be discouraged by your doubts or frustrations.
God knows that following him isn't always easy. He is not
dismayed by your stumbling blocks. Instead, every tiny step
you take toward him brings him great joy.

God, thank you for the power and privilege of faith. I love
you, believe in you, and rejoice in your goodness. Strengthen
my faith and help me follow you closely.

REST SECURELY

My heart is glad and my tongue rejoices;
my body also will rest secure.

PSALM 16:9 NIV

One of God's greatest gifts to us is peace. We give him our worries, and he takes care of them. When we are burdened by the weight of our anxieties, we can take them directly to Jesus. We rejoice in the freedom we experience, and we can rest knowing that we are taken care of. There is no need to ruminate on intrusive thoughts when God offers us peace that surpasses understanding.

God's peace is all-inclusive. It provides security for your soul, mental reprieve, and physical rest for your body. Each of these things is important; God does not overlook any of them. He knows exactly what you need in each area of your life, and he is fully capable of providing it. Take a deep breath and let his peace infiltrate every corner of your heart and mind. Rejoice in the Lord, for there is rest and security available to you in his tender care.

Jesus, when my body is exhausted, and my nerves are on edge, I need the power of your peace. Settle my heart and help me relax in your presence. Flood me with peace and give me the rest I need.

Full of Joy

"You shall go out in joy
and be led forth in peace;
the mountains and the hills before you
shall break forth into singing,
and all the trees of the field shall clap their hands."

ISAIAH 55:12 ESV

When we follow the Lord, our lives are marked by joy and peace. We don't rely on our own understanding, but we trust his wise perspective. Our knowledge is limited, but his knowledge is expansive. There is peace for those who trust in him, and there is joy for all who delight in him! Following him is not meant to be drudgery. There is an abundance of goodness in his presence.

Surely, you will experience suffering in your lifetime. It's unavoidable and inevitable. There will be difficult days and seasons of heartbreak. However, your relationship with God is not meant to be one of those trials. He is your source of joy and peace. You aren't meant to be a martyr in every situation of your life. Go to God with confidence and expect that he will give you the gift of joy when you ask.

Wonderful One, you lead me along pleasant paths, and you restore my joy. I trust you to continue to guide me in your goodness all the days of my life.

Clear Insight

The commandments of the LORD are right,
bringing joy to the heart.
The commands of the LORD are clear,
giving insight for living.

PSALM 19:8 NLT

God delights in leading his children. He wants us to experience his goodness, and he loves revealing the clarity of his wisdom to those who look for it. If we want shortcuts to worldly success, we won't find them with him. But if we want the path to a meaningful and satisfying life, he is the one who provides it. His ways are always best.

While following God requires perseverance, it is not complicated. God offers clear insight and wisdom anytime you need it. It is not his desire that you flounder through life, unable to make concise decisions. He does not want your thoughts to be jumbled or for you to feel inadequate. If you ask, he will direct you faithfully on the path that leads to eternal life. He will keep you steady and secure no matter what is happening around you.

Wise God, your ways are better than mine, and your thoughts are higher than mine. I want my life to be defined by your wisdom. Help me trust you and follow you closely.

NOURISHING WORDS

Your words were found and I ate them,
And Your words became a joy to me
and the delight of my heart;
For I have been called by Your name,
LORD God of armies.

JEREMIAH 15:16 NASB

When God speaks to us, it is full of wisdom, clarity, and love. Jeremiah found the Words of God and he digested them. They gave him joy, and they filled his heart with delight. They nourished his soul. The same God who spoke to Jeremiah speaks to us still. We can open our Bibles and read his instructions. We can listen to the guidance and prompting of the Holy Spirit. We can listen to the wisdom of others inspired by God.

Take note of how Jeremiah viewed God's Words. He consumed them and soaked them in. He recognized that they were valuable to his life. He didn't brush them off or glaze over them. God's Word is meant to have a profound impact on your life. He has given them to you as a gift, and you would be wise to take advantage of it. Soften your heart and let God's Word filter into your life steadily and poignantly.

Lord, speak to me today. Encourage me with your Word. I trust you to open my ears so I can hear your voice. Expand my mind to understand your ways. Your Word is life to me!

OVERFLOWING DELIGHT

"Now I am returning to you so Father,
I pray that they will experience
and enter into my joyous delight
in you so that it is fulfilled in them and overflows."

JOHN 17:13 TPT

Jesus delights in God, and God delights in him. Their relationship is joyous and lovely. Through Christ's death on the cross, we have the same access to the Father as he does. We can experience the same delight and wonder that he talks about in Scripture. We can be filled to overflowing with the joyous delight that comes from knowing the Father.

Of all the requirements you might put on yourself, have you ever considered that God wants you to be joyful? It's easy to assume that he wants you to be disciplined, pure, holy, patient, or long-suffering. While those are all good things, don't forget that he also wants you to be full of joy! His desire is for you to have an abundant life and to experience the full depth of his goodness.

God, I want to experience your delight! Fill me with joy and show me more of your goodness. Thank you for being so kind and wonderful.

It Is Possible

Our hearts ache, but we always have joy.
We are poor, but we give spiritual riches to others.
We own nothing, and yet we have everything.

2 CORINTHIANS 6:10 NLT

More than one thing can be true at the same time. We can be grateful for a situation yet still desire change. We can be deep in grief and also be delighted by ordinary things. We can be disappointed and yet still hold on to hope. We do not have to choose one or the other. Opposing forces coexist in and around us. It's normal to hold varying emotions and situations simultaneously.

No matter what your circumstances are, God is with you. He offers you the fullness of his presence and resources. Especially in seasons of loss, it is helpful to remember that mercy and redemption are abundant in God's kingdom. Your situation does not dictate God's love, power, or plans. He is greater than all the troubles you will ever face. You can rejoice, for he is faithful and will help you navigate even the most complex situation.

God, I rely on you during the hard days and cling to you during the good ones. You are the same, no matter what changes in my life. Let me experience the goodness of your presence today.

WITHOUT BLAME

In Christ, he chose us before the world was made so that we would be his holy people—people without blame before him.

EPHESIANS 1:4 NCV

We all fall short of the glory of God. We know our limitations and are well acquainted with our failures. Perfection is a goal that is out of our reach. Yet, even with our faults and flaws, Christ's grace is abundant. His mercy covers our sins and removes our guilt! When we humble ourselves before Jesus, he pays the price for our sins. He has made us blameless before God, not by anything we have done but solely by the power of his mercy.

God doesn't look at you and see a failure. He sees his beloved child. Even when you struggle, he is tender toward you. Don't hesitate another moment to repair the rift that has kept you from him. As you offer your mistakes to him, he will overwhelm you with his mercy. He will set you on the right path and free you from shame.

Merciful God, thank you for being so kind! I'm so glad my mistakes don't keep me from your presence. I bring you all of me. Meet me with mercy yet again.

Paths in Life

You have revealed the paths of life to me;
you will fill me with gladness
in your presence.

ACTS 2:28 CSB

When we seek God earnestly, we will find him. When our highest priority is bringing him honor, our life will be an act of worship toward him. We will steadily walk the path of life when keep our eyes securely on him. It can be easy for our Christian walk to become more of a trudge. We focus on our failures and lament how hard it is to navigate a broken world. This is not God's desire for us. We are meant to experience the gladness of his presence while we wait for his return.

The unique journey you are on looks different from those around you. You have different challenges, trials, and joys than anyone else. You aren't meant to walk through a cookie cutter version of life. As a believer, however, you are meant to experience the gladness of his presence no matter what your circumstances are. No matter what your path looks like, God wants you to be blessed by his nearness. While the scenery of your life may differ, your eyes are meant to be fixed on the Lord along with every other believer.

Faithful One, fill me with gladness in your presence today. I trust you with my future. Lead me while I travel the pathways of life. I embrace your fellowship today.

Spend Time

If you have any encouragement from being united with
Christ, if any comfort from his love, if any common sharing
in the Spirit, if any tenderness and compassion, then make
my joy complete by being like-minded, having the same love,
being one in spirit and of one mind.

PHILIPPIANS 2:1-2 NIV

We become like the people with whom we associate. As
we spend time with people, we rub off on each other. This is
why we should be intentional about our close relationships,
and that includes our relationship with Christ. The more
time we spend with Jesus the more we will resemble his
character. As we get to know him, his character rubs off on
us and we grow in love, compassion, and joy.

If you want to be more like Jesus spend time with him.
Sit in his presence. Study the Word. Listen to the guidance of
the Holy Spirit. Let his love transform you. As you are united
with him, you will begin to reflect who he is. Be encouraged
knowing that becoming like Christ doesn't mean perfection
but maturing in the ability to love others well.

*Lord, I want to be more like you. Help me love others well. As
I spend time with you, teach me how to reflect your love to
those around me.*

Restorer

He makes me lie down in green pastures.
He leads me beside still waters.
He restores my soul.
He leads me in paths of righteousness
for his name's sake.

PSALM 23:2-3 ESV

We've all met people whose presence is refreshing
and life-giving. What is it about them that makes us feel
rejuvenated? Perhaps they listen without judgment. Maybe
they offer timely advice to encourage and give hope.
Whatever the reason, being around them feels easy and like a
sweet gift. This is how we are meant to feel in God's presence.
He wants to give good gifts to his children. He isn't waiting
for us to come to him so he can berate us or make sure we
know everything we've done wrong.

God always knows what you need at any given time. He
sees you in your struggles and he offers rest from the worries
of life. He invites you to follow him and escape the noises
of the world. He restores you with the peacefulness of his
presence. What do you need rest from today? What do you
need restored? Follow the Shepherd as he leads you; you will
find what you need today.

*God, lead me into peace, refreshment, and rest today. Give me
fresh hope and help me lean on you when I need a break.*

Overcomers

Every child of God defeats this evil world,
and we achieve this victory through our faith.

1 John 5:4 nlt

As God's children, we are overcomers of this world. We don't use brute force or the strength of our own will. Instead, we rely fully on the undeserved grace of God. God helps us become resilient as we lean on him to help us through the hard times. We overcome the evil in the world by living in the ways of God's kingdom. God consistently leads us with love, peace, and wisdom.

Whether you find yourself in a calm season or one of testing and hard work, you can trust that Christ will get you through. There is nothing he cannot overcome. Jesus came to give you abundant life and a direct connection to the Father. You have access to the Father in every season, no matter what the circumstances of your life are. Today, utilize the overcoming power of Christ's victory as you walk through your day.

Jesus, you are the way, the truth, and the life. You have made me a conqueror of fear, sin, and evil through the power of your merciful love. Thank you!

DEEP WELL

The LORD is my strength and my shield;
My heart trusts in Him, and I am helped;
Therefore my heart triumphs,
And with my song I shall thank Him.

PSALM 28:7 NASB

There are days we seem to question everything. It's normal to experience doubt and frustration at different points of life. The drudgery of day-to-day activities can keep us from seeing the bigger picture. There are times when we put the work in, but not much seems to change. Those are the moments we need fortitude and perseverance to keep trusting God. If truth is deeply rooted in our hearts, we will have a well to draw from when we are discouraged.

The Lord is your strength. When you feel weak, God's gracious power is available to you. The Lord is your shield. He protects you from harm, and he keeps you safe. As you continue to trust God, he will prove his faithfulness over and over! The more you believe in the truth of the Word, the stronger you will be when trials arise.

Faithful One, thank you for helping me with all I need. Let truth be firmly established in my heart and help me continuously lean on you for strength.

From the Well

With joy you will draw water
From the wells of salvation.

ISAIAH 12:3 NKJV

Our salvation is like a well of fresh spring water. We can draw on it when we are tired, thirsty, or overwhelmed. It has the power to bring refreshment and delight to our lives. Through Christ's work on the cross, we have complete and constant access to the life-giving presence of the Father. We have gleaned the eternal benefits of Jesus' sacrifice.

God has led you out of the captivity of shame and fear. He has given you a path away from the guilt of sin and into the liberty of his love. You are free in his mercy to sing, dance, and shout for joy! When you come to the Father through Jesus Christ, there is fulfilling peace, perfect love, and complete joy. What hope you have in the glorious goodness of his presence!

Lord, I come to you with an open heart, drawing from the well of salvation with pleasure and joy. Thank you for the abundance of life I find in you today!

Every Promise

The Lord Yahweh, Commander of Angel Armies,
makes this solemn decree:
"Be sure of this: Just as I have planned, so it will be.
Every purpose of my heart will surely come to pass."

ISAIAH 14:24 TPT

We don't have to strive to make God's promises happen. His ability to do what he says has nothing to do with our actions. His mercy has no end, and his love cannot be deterred! His intentions will not be thrown off course. No matter what we do or think, the purposes of God's heart will surely come to pass. We get to rest knowing that our work isn't necessary.

When you build your confidence upon the true and faithful nature of God, you will remain steady and secure. Though many things shift and shake in this world, you can depend on the powerful character of God which remains steadfast through it all. What God has set in motion will be completed. You can trust him to do it! Let your worries fall aside and lean on God's promise to follow through with his plans.

Mighty God, you are the ultimate promise keeper. You are not fickle, and you do not change your mind. You are true, faithful, and kind.

GOD'S PEOPLE REJOICE

He brought his people out with rejoicing,
his chosen ones with shouts of joy.

PSALM 105:43 CSB

We often neglect to celebrate victories or noteworthy achievements. Rejoicing is an act of celebration, but it is also a discipline we must cultivate. We are so quick to move on to the next thing. We are quite good at celebrating big milestones, but we aren't very good at joyfully acknowledging the little successes in our lives.

You can rejoice in completing a project that took a while to accomplish. You can rejoice when your kids get through an afternoon without arguing. You can rejoice when you master a new skill or check a task off your to do list. Rejoicing may not come easily, but the more we practice it the more natural it is to celebrate with those around us. It is good to thank God for any and every good thing in your life.

Lord, open my eyes so I can practice the joy of celebration in little and big ways. Teach me to recognize each moment that points to God's blessings.

Every Good Action

Every good action and every perfect gift is from God. These good gifts come down from the Creator of the sun, moon, and stars, who does not change like their shifting shadows.

JAMES 1:17 NCV

The kindness of others is a gift from God. Every act of mercy reflects our Father. When we expect a harsh reaction and are met with a gentle tone, it's a reminder of the great love that God has for us. God is patient, offering us more than enough grace in every moment. It's beautiful when we receive this love through the actions of others!

When you consider the gifts God has given you, don't forget the way other people have shown you his love. All goodness originates in God and reflects his love is at work. You can see glimpses of his glory in the people around you. Your life may be full of material blessings, but don't forget to praise God for how other people have impacted you. The good actions of others are as much a gift as the food on your table.

Father, thank you for filling my life with good gifts. Help me notice the good actions of others. I praise you for the way I've seen your love displayed by the people around me.

Grateful Acceptance

Everything God created is good, and nothing is to be
rejected if it is received with thanksgiving.

1 TIMOTHY 4:4 NIV

There are many religious traditions that put strict
parameters on what people can eat. Though there is nothing
wrong with putting parameters on our own diets, it becomes
a stumbling block when we use it as a tool of judgment.
Setting up little rules for ourselves is a slippery slope. Over
time, it's easy to view certain habits as the parameters for our
salvation.

Christ set you free from the requirements of the law.
You are now bound only to the lavish love of God. There is
no rule you can follow that will give you right standing with
God. Instead of striving to meet an impossible standard, you
are free to rely on his mercy and grace. He doesn't want your
life to be full of anxiety. He doesn't want you to constantly
wonder if you're good enough. God has blessed you with
freedom and a full pardon. Remain thankful and live in
response to his gift.

*Gracious God, remove any religious guilt I am carrying. Help
me walk in freedom, trusting only in your grace. I want my
life to be a response to what you've already done for me. Keep
me from the trap of striving for my salvation.*

HAND-IN-HAND

Trust in the Lord, and do good;
dwell in the land and befriend faithfulness.

PSALM 37:3 ESV

Faith and actions go hand-in-hand. When we trust in the Lord, we don't opt out of our own responsibility to live in a way that honors him. We lean on him fully for the undeserved mercy of salvation. From that place of abundant grace, we make choices that reflect his character and desire for our lives. We are called to trust in the Lord *and* do good.

The way you live matters. Your actions do not dictate God's mercy, but they are evidence of his grace in your life. When you insist that nothing you do matters, you forfeit the true freedom found in living God's way. Conversely, when you put your own goodness on a pedestal, you forfeit the true rest found in surrendering to God's mercy. The balance of these two things is the dance of the Christian life. The good news is that you are perfectly equipped to do it well.

Lord Jesus, you are the best example of trusting in God. I want to lean on your grace, and I want to please you with my thoughts and actions. Help me honor you in all I do.

The Light of Life

This light within you produces
only what is good and right and true.

EPHESIANS 5:9 NLT

Goodness, righteousness, and truth shine brightly in those who yield their lives to the Lord. Just like the stars and the moon reflect the brilliant light of the sun, we reflect the character of God. When we choose to follow him, we bear the fruit of the Spirit living within us. We continuously lay down our fleshly desires and surrender to living in a way that honors God.

God is doing good things in your life. He is consistently at work, and he is not finished with you. As you follow him, you can be confident that he is at work even when you don't realize it. He will produce fruit within you that is good, right, and true. If you are dissatisfied with parts of your life, you can trust that it is never too late to see change. Without a doubt, God's work in your life doesn't operate within your perceived timeline.

My Creator, I am in awe of how you move in this world. Thank you for your faithful work in my life. Help me trust that your light will produce good things within me.

JUNE

You delight in showing
unfailing love.

MICAH 7:18 NLT

His Presence

The Lord passed by in front of him and proclaimed,
"The Lord, the Lord God, compassionate and merciful,
slow to anger, and abounding in faithfulness and truth."

EXODUS 34:6 NASB

God's nature cannot be separated from his presence.
When we are with him, we will experience the goodness
of everything he is. Wherever he goes there is compassion,
mercy, patience, faithfulness, and truth. These things are
evidence that God is at work. His presence is not simply
conceptual or something we need to over spiritualize.

If you look at your life, there are likely several areas
where God is at work. Where there is evidence of his
character, he is moving. Have you noticed yourself being more
patient, servant-hearted, or compassionate? God is moving
in your life. Where he goes, goodness follows. Don't despair
if there are times you don't feel his presence in the way you
expect. He is always moving, and he is always nearby.

*Lord, it is delightful to know you! Your character is reliable,
and everything you do is good. Help me see evidence of your
love in my life. Show me more of who you are.*

In the Details

"Don't worry. For your Father cares deeply about
even the smallest detail of your life."

MATTHEW 10:30-31 TPT

Little worries can become big burdens if we don't learn
to lay them aside. Jesus encouraged his followers to let go
of their worries. That invitation remains open to each of us
today. God is aware of each sparrow that falls from its nest.
He is also aware of every detail of our lives. There is nothing
he doesn't see. He is mindful toward us, and he loves to care
for his children.

What details are you prone to worry over? Which cares
take up the most space in your mind? You can confidently
surrender each one of them over to God. He is fully capable
of carrying all your burdens. He knows exactly what you
need even before you are aware of it. You can trust him to
provide for you. He is not too busy to take notice of you, and
he is not ill equipped to help you. He is a loving Father who
will faithfully care for you.

*Faithful Father, thank you for being at work in the details
of my life. I trust you to provide what I need. Thank you for
being so attentive and kind. Open my eyes to your presence in
my life.*

Go in Peace

Jesus said to them again, "Peace to you!
As the Father has sent Me, I also send you."

JOHN 20:21 NKJV

Jesus humbly came to the world to reconcile us to the Father. His entire life was dedicated to giving us a glimpse of what his Father's house looks like. He explained the principles of the kingdom, and he taught us about God's character. Every word he spoke proclaimed the goodness and everlasting love of our heavenly Father.

Jesus is a perfect reflection of God, and he calls you to be the same. Just like Jesus, you are meant to declare God's goodness to the world. Your words and actions should be founded on the principles of the kingdom of heaven. There is no need to be intimidated by Christ's commission because you've been fully equipped by the Holy Spirit. As you seek to share God's love with others, you are never alone.

God, thank you for your constant presence. Give me courage, peace, and compassion as I try to share your love with others. I want to teach others about the goodness of your character.

Good Thoughts

Brothers and sisters, think about the things that are good and worthy of praise. Think about the things that are true and honorable and right and pure and beautiful and respected.

PHILIPPIANS 4:8 NCV

It can be discouraging when we think about something we aren't proud of. Thankfully, we don't have to feel shame about the thoughts that come to us. We do have to take responsibility for the direction they take. We can't always control everything that flashes across our minds, but we can control what we dwell on. We can cultivate the discipline of aligning our thoughts with what is good and right.

If you approach your thoughts with curiosity and compassion, you can more easily steer them toward the things that are good and worthy of praise. Furthermore, it is good to be intentional about what you ingest—the things you watch, listen to, and partake of. Your thought life is likely a direct result of the influences in your life. If you want your thoughts to be honorable and beautiful, you'll need to pursue that which is honorable and beautiful.

Holy One, thank you for your Holy Spirit who helps me manage my thoughts. Give me grace to pursue what is good and right. I want my thoughts and actions to honor you.

Encouraged to Hope

God has given both his promise and his oath. These two things are unchangeable because it is impossible for God to lie. Therefore, we who have fled to him for refuge can have great confidence as we hold to the hope that lies before us.

HEBREWS 6:17-18 NLT

We have all been disappointed by others. Even the most well-intentioned people can fail to keep their promises. Our understanding of the concept of oaths is limited by our humanity. When we think of God and his ability to keep a promise, we have to be careful not to apply our own disappointments to his character. Even though we can't always comprehend it, God's word cannot be broken under any circumstances. He will never disappoint us.

God encourages you to take hold of the hope he has set before you. You can be perfectly sure that he will never change his mind. His mercy is yours forever. Success is promised. It is absolute. Let your faith be strengthened knowing that God's promise to you is unshakeable. God is your salvation and strength. You can depend on him fully, and you can trust him with great abandon. He will not let you down.

Lord, my hope is in you. Thank you for being unshakeable and unchanging. I am so thankful for your steadfast love.

Space to Rest

He brought me out into a spacious place;
he rescued me because he delighted in me.

2 Samuel 22:20 niv

God's love leads him to do more for us than we can envision. He has offered us salvation through his Son, and he gives us space to rest, heal, and thrive. There is no need for us to carry the weight of our sin, anxieties, or stress. God offers to take our burdens and gives us peace in exchange. In his presence we can take a deep breath, let our worries fade, and relax into the comfort of his love.

Think about a time when God rescued you. Perhaps no one else even knew what you were suffering, but God in his faithfulness miraculously helped you. He did this because he was delighted with you. He will help you again because he still delights in you! No matter how often you need him, he will always be there. Trust in him, for he is faithful and true.

Lord, lead me into a spacious place where I can regain my footing in your peaceful presence. Help me know how deeply you delight in me, so I can confidently rest in your love.

GODLY WISDOM

"My child, listen to what I say,
and treasure my commands.
Tune your ears to wisdom,
and concentrate on understanding."

PROVERBS 2:1-2 NLT

If we are wise, we will direct our attention to what God says. We will listen to his voice with the expectation that what he says is good and right. If we are wise, we will choose to trust his leadership and search for his ways like a hidden treasure. When we focus our energy and resources on doing what he lovingly guides us to do, then we will understand what it is to fear the Lord.

Devote your life to the pursuit of Godly wisdom and you will not be disappointed. There is great value in reading God's Word and allowing it to filter through every aspect of your life. Nothing on this earth will satisfy you like the knowledge and understanding found in the Lord. His ways are far more valuable than anything else you could spend your time pursuing. Today, adjust your priorities and seek the unmatched treasure of godly wisdom.

God, I want to pursue wisdom all of my days. I want your knowledge and understanding to be my own. When I am distracted by worldly pursuits, gently draw me back to you. Help me listen to your voice and respond to what you say.

Fullness of Life

May you experience the love of Christ, though it is too great
to understand fully. Then you will be made complete with all
the fullness of life and power that comes from God.

EPHESIANS 3:19 NLT

The love of God is not something we learn simply by
reading about it. We don't reach a certification level, pass
all our exams, or prove we know it all. The love of the Lord
is too vast to pin down. It is too grand to describe. Today's
verse encourages us to truly experience the love of Christ. It
is meant to be felt, accepted, lived, and offered to others.

The fullness of life comes from the experience of God's
love! That should excite and encourage you! Understanding
his love is a continual experience that is available to you for
your entire life. Each day you can draw from the strength of
his love. Let it fill your heart and allow you to move through
your day with security and confidence.

*God, thank you for the power of your love. I would be lost
without it. Give me grace to seek you each morning. I want to
experience the fullness of life that comes from you.*

Soul-Satisfying Goodness

They shall give thanks to the Lord for His mercy,
And for His wonders to the sons of mankind!
For He has satisfied the thirsty soul,
And He has filled the hungry soul with what is good.

Psalm 107:8-9 NASB

The mercies of God are remarkable and satisfying. He is truly better than we give him credit for. He is eternally kind and is worthy of all our praise. He fills our soul with goodness, and he does not leave us wanting. He loves to give good gifts to his children. Devoting our lives to God does not mean that we must forsake delight and satisfaction. Rather, it's an understanding that only he can satisfy the deepest longings of our souls.

If you have a thirst in your heart or a hunger in your soul that you cannot fill, go to the Lord. He offers soul satisfaction and heart nourishment. His love will never fail, and it is his desire that you would experience the goodness of his presence. No matter what your soul craves, God can meet it. His resources are endless, and his generosity is great.

Lord, I humble my heart before you today. I long for a fresh taste of your kindness and a deeper experience of your goodness. Thank you for all you've done for me.

Anywhere and Everywhere

The Lord loves seeing justice on the earth.
Anywhere and everywhere you can
find his faithful, unfailing love!

PSALM 33:5 TPT

The world is filled with evidence of God's faithful, unfailing love! Every landscape and corner of the earth testifies to his goodness. Not one city or village is absent of God's faithful mercy. Everywhere we look, we can find examples of God's perfection. His work is all around us, and he is worthy of our praise.

When was the last time you looked for evidence of God's mercy in your community? No matter how discouraging the state of the world is, don't lose sight of the goodness that is present. God is always at work even when you don't understand or can't quite see it. His love never fails, and his faithfulness has no end. Even when it feels hopeless or dark, take notice of how God's sustaining love is at work.

Faithful One, there is no darkness you cannot shine your light on. Help me see evidence of your love even when I am overwhelmed or hopeless. Renew your Spirit within me and help me pay attention to the way are moving in my life.

The Tide Turns

He will yet fill your mouth with laughing,
And your lips with rejoicing.

JOB 8:21 NKJV

On hard days it can be difficult to remember that our whole existence isn't permeated by suffering. There are painful seasons in life, and we cannot escape them. However, we can know the power of God's blessed presence in each and every one. Do we need a dash of hope today? Do we long for a fresh portion of peace? Just like the dawn brings light and hope, so God brings us out of the dark nights of the soul. The tide will turn, and a new day will come.

If there is breath in your lungs today, you have not reached the end of your life. You have not experienced the fullness of all God has planned for you. No matter what you are going through, or have faced in the past, God is not finished. He will continue sowing mercy into the details of your life. He promises that you will still laugh and be filled with rejoicing. You can depend on this. Your future isn't doomed, and God is not finished with you.

Merciful One, thank you for the encouragement of your presence and the power of your mercy. You bring redemption to seemingly hopeless situations. Meet me and remind me of your goodness.

No Fear

God did not give us a spirit that makes us afraid
but a spirit of power and love and self-control.

2 Timothy 1:7 NCV

When fear is our motivation, we struggle to remain
open and flexible. When we operate out of fear, we forfeit
the ability to see anything other than perceived threats. Fear
restricts our decision-making abilities, and it can make us
irritable and anxious. The Spirit of God does not motivate us
with fear. The Spirit gives us strength, love, and self-restraint.

When you choose fear over the power of the Holy
Spirit, you miss the peace that is freely offered to you. There
is nothing forcing you to live in fear. By your own volition,
you can choose to be bound to all the Spirit offers instead.
Prayerfully seek the Lord. Fill your mind with Scripture. Rest
in the promises God has made. Nothing stands between you
and the abundance of his love.

*God, I don't want to live in fear. You have given me freedom
from the power of sin and death. Help me cling to your
promises instead of living like a slave to fear.*

Greater Strength

You are from God, little children, and you have conquered
them, because the one who is in you is greater than the one
who is in the world.

1 John 4:4 csb

It can feel as if we are walking a lonely path when we
choose to follow God instead of chasing our own successes.
It is tempting to search for gratification in this life instead of
trusting in the promise of future perfection. However, the
pursuit of God is worth it because nothing satisfies the way
his all-consuming love does. Though the ways of the world
can be both tempting and discouraging, God has overcome
the world, and he is worth our pursuit.

Whatever struggle you are having, either with others or
internally, God's presence can guide you through. You are
not fighting a losing battle. Christ has already empowered
you to overcome. He has claimed eternal victory through the
cross, and he has not forsaken you to face the world on your
own. He is on your side, and he is fully capable of fighting
your battles.

*Gracious Father, I need your help every day. Each battle I face
feels overwhelming and discouraging. Give me strength and
help me rely on you.*

PROTECT YOUR HEART

Above all else, guard your heart,
for everything you do flows from it.

PROVERBS 4:23 NIV

It's common to combine the subject of guarding our hearts with the subject of purity. We often think about keeping ourselves undefiled by worldly culture or impure influences. As such, we may be hyper-vigilant about obvious issues. We might be wary of films with immoral content or other media with questionable morals. It's certainly good to avoid problematic influences but we should be more worried about the Holy Spirit's leadership than our own idea of right and wrong.

It's easy to make rules and follow them. It's harder to follow the Holy Spirit's consistent guidance. He wants to protect your heart from more than what's obvious. He may prompt you to be wary of bitterness, anxiety, or jealousy. These things can be just as damaging as the stereotypical issues we tend to talk about. No matter what guarding your heart looks like in your life, trust the Holy Spirit to guide you.

God, please help me guard my heart. Help me obey the guidance of the Holy Spirit. Open my ears to hear your voice and help me make wise choices.

He Attends to You

You know when I sit down and when I rise up;
you discern my thoughts from afar.

PSALM 139:2 ESV

God knows when we lay our head down at night and when we get up each morning. He recognizes our thoughts, and he hears our prayers. We have our Father's attention. He lovingly cares for each of us, and he delights when we turn to him for help. He is not only attentive, but he is fully equipped to provide us with everything we need.

God knows you through and through, and he loves you more than you can imagine. His grace is abundant, and he will meet you where you are weak. Invite him into your day and ask him to reveal his kindness to you in a fresh way. He sees you, and he is not discouraged or worried about your life. He has a beautiful plan for you, and you can trust that he will fulfill his purposes for you!

Father, you see me even when I feel isolated or overlooked by others. Thank you for loving me and drawing me into your presence over and over again.

Encouraging Presence

"This is my command—be strong and courageous!
Do not be afraid or discouraged.
For the LORD your God is with you wherever you go."

JOSHUA 1:9 NLT

God is our strength, courage, and hope. He promises to never leave us, and we can trust that he will adhere to his word. What he has said, he will do. What he vows, he fulfills. He is loyal in love, and he is faithful in truth. When he tells us to be strong it isn't because he expects us to will our way into obedience. He tells us to be strong because he has equipped us, and he will help us. His strength is what makes us courageous.

Today, hold on to the promise that God is with you wherever you go. You are never alone. You may come up against challenges today, but you can be strong and courageous in the knowledge that God is with you. He has all the solutions to any problems that arise. He is wise in every situation. Trust him and lean into his presence.

God, thank you for your presence. It's so reassuring that I don't have to do anything alone. You are with me even when I don't feel like you are. May my confidence be in your strength over my own.

WAIT PATIENTLY

Those who wait for the LORD
Will gain new strength;
They will mount up with wings like eagles,
They will run and not get tired,
They will walk and not become weary.

ISAIAH 40:31 NASB

Instant gratification does not grow patience. Patience is a quality that must be intentionally pursued. Our culture feeds us instant answers, ready resources, and connections to people at any hour. There's endless entertainment to consume, countless ways to distract us, and people selling us solutions to every problem. While we all like the benefits of these things, they certainly are not helping us develop patience or long suffering.

Wisdom calls you to practice patience. You may have to fight the urge to consume what the world has to offer. Instead of clicking your way to satisfaction, you can create room in your life for the benefits of waiting. As you discipline your flesh, you may find that you don't even want what you thought would make you happy. Saying no to immediate gratification may result in you seeking the Lord and finding the true satisfaction you crave.

Lord God, help me build space into my life for waiting and patience. Help me lean on you in all that I do.

Keep Coming Back

Be my strong refuge,
To which I may resort continually;
You have given the commandment to save me,
For You are my rock and my fortress.

PSALM 71:3 NKJV

God is not a one-time helper in times of trouble. We can go to him whenever we need him. He is our refuge in any and every difficulty. His presence is our strength and our peace. We never need to suffer in silence or in isolation. He welcomes us with open arms every time we come to him.

Have you ever felt as if you have worn out your welcome with someone? Maybe you feel that if you aren't careful, God may get tired of you. The truth is God is delighted by you at all times. He has an open-door policy with all his beloved children. You don't have to stay away and save his help for a rainy day. You have it whenever you need it!

Lord, you are my strong refuge, and I come to you today. Bless me with your peaceful presence and strengthen me in your powerful love. I rest in you and lean on your strength.

Cascading Peace

May grace and perfect peace cascade over you as you live in the rich knowledge of God and of Jesus our Lord.

2 Peter 1:2 tpt

Grace is the unmerited favor of God and the foundation of our salvation. Only by God's grace are we redeemed. Everything we believe is built upon grace, and without it we are left to strive for something we can never attain. As we learn more about who God is and seek to apply truth to our lives, we will continue to experience his grace in abundance.

When you live in the knowledge of God, he will satisfy your every need. He asks you to follow him, and then he fills your life with rich blessings. Grace and peace will flow over you like a waterfall. Each day, as you look to him, he will pour out his favor upon you. He sees your devotion, and he meets you with unlimited grace and peace.

Heavenly Father, increase my knowledge of who you are. Help me follow you faithfully. I need the power of your peace and the strength of your grace. Fill me to overflowing.

MUCH TO LEARN

Everything that was written in the past was written to teach us. The Scriptures give us patience and encouragement so that we can have hope.

ROMANS 15:4 NCV

At first glance, it's easy to be intimidated by the great examples of faith we see in Scripture. We may think we'll never be as brave as David or as wise as Solomon. We may never be as devoted as Mary or as faithful as Paul. We often look at these people and put them up on a pedestal. When we focus only on their victories, we do ourselves a disservice. Each person mentioned in the Word was just as human as we are. They had just as many struggles and were equally lost in sin.

No one is perfect, yet God moves through the weaknesses of those who trust and surrender to him. The Word was not given to you as an impossible standard you cannot meet. There is no need to be discouraged or intimidated by the examples of faith you see. Instead, they are there to teach you and give you hope. You can learn just as much from their failures as you can from their success.

Faithful God, encourage me as I read the Word today. Teach me more about who you are. I trust you will give me wisdom and hope when I need it most.

Suffer Courageously

"I have told you these things so that in me you may have peace. You will have suffering in this world. Be courageous! I have conquered the world."

JOHN 16:33 CSB

No one wants to suffer or live in pain. Yet, we know it is inevitable. We will experience loss, grief, and trauma. Our bodies will deteriorate, and our minds may fail. Our experiences cannot be predicted or perfectly outlined. The only thing we can truly rely on is the faithfulness of Jesus. No matter what shifting sands we walk through, he remains steady and secure. When everything is shaking, we can find peace in the reliability of Christ.

When you encounter times of suffering, it is not because you have failed. Painful experiences are inevitable in this fallen world. Your hope is not meant to be based on comfort or the outward circumstances of your life. As a follower of Christ, you are not promised an easy life. You are promised undeserved salvation and the promise of eternity in the presence of God. Let that truth be your anchor in difficult seasons. Lean on God's faithfulness, and trust that he will never leave you.

Lord Jesus, I don't want to lose hope when I suffer. Establish me in your love. I trust you for comfort and encouragement no matter what I am going through.

God of Comfort

Praise be to the God and Father of our Lord Jesus Christ,
the Father of compassion and the God of all comfort, who
comforts us in all our troubles, so that we can comfort those in
any trouble with the comfort we ourselves receive from God.

2 Corinthians 1:3-4 niv

Comfort is an expression of kindness. God's comfort
reveals the power of his love for us. He is patient, kind, and
thoughtful. He is tenderhearted and gentle with our pain. He
does not rush our grief or tell us not to mourn. He meets us
in the darkest depths of our sorrow. He comes close when we
are hurting and sits with us in the midst of our heartbreak.

Grief is a complicated emotion that is difficult to gauge.
Let God manage the tangled mess you are feeling. Let him
meet you with tenderness and compassion. You can trust
that he will treat you with the utmost care. As you realize
how incredibly gentle he is with your pain, you will learn
to treat others the same way. It might take some time, but
eventually God's kindness toward you will overflow to those
around you.

*God, thank you for your comfort and compassion. I am so
grateful for your tender care. Sit with me while I mourn and
meet me in my pain. I trust you with the most vulnerable
parts of my heart.*

PILGRIMAGE

What joy for those whose strength comes from the LORD,
who have set their minds on a pilgrimage to Jerusalem.

PSALM 84:5 NLT

The purpose of a pilgrimage is found fully in the
destination. The meaning of the trip is not in the journey or
what might be seen along the way. When someone goes on a
pilgrimage it's because they are trying to get to an extremely
specific place. All that matters is what will be found at the
end of the road. The desire to get there is so strong that the
pilgrim will endure all manner of difficulties to ensure they
complete their journey.

When Scripture says that you are on a pilgrimage to
Jerusalem it is a picture of your journey toward eternity.
Your highest goal is to spend all your days in the perfect
presence of God. Like a pilgrim, you can gain strength and
motivation from the end destination. When you know what
you are working toward, you will faithfully move forward.
No matter what happens along the way, don't look to the
left or the right. Keep your eyes steadily on the prize that is
eternal oneness with your Maker.

*Lord, you are my strength. My hope is in you, and I look
forward to spending eternity in your presence. Equip me to walk
steadily all the days of my life. Keep my eyes focused on you.*

Your Needs

We also pray that you will be strengthened with all his
glorious power so you will have all the endurance and
patience you need. May you be filled with joy.

COLOSSIANS 1:11 NLT

Our soul needs as much strengthening as our body
does. In some cases, even more so. It doesn't matter how
much outer strength we have if we lack it internally. We
can't strong arm our way through conflicts, and we can't grit
our teeth through trials. What we really need is endurance,
patience, and joy. These things come directly from the divine
power of God. He is the one who gives us what we need to
face the day.

When conflict arises in your life, what does your typical
arsenal consist of? Maybe you focus on pampering yourself
to find comfort. Maybe you meet problems head on with the
strength of your will. Maybe you try your best to hide until
it's all over. No matter what your tendencies are, what you
really need is for God to strengthen your spirit. He is the
only one who can give you what you need. Lean on him and
trust that he will equip you with endurance, patience, and
joy when you need it most.

*God, I need your help today. Give me the endurance I need
to make it through each trial I face. Thank you for being so
faithful and kind.*

HE'S NOT FINISHED

I am confident of this very thing,
that He who began a good work among you
will complete it by the day of Christ Jesus.

PHILIPPIANS 1:6 NASB

God is faithful in every season and in every circumstance. No matter how many times we trip and fall, God's presence is reliable, and his love is loyal. He doesn't give up on us, so let's not give up on ourselves either. As long as we draw breath on this earth, his mercy and redemption will be available. He lovingly restores what we cannot, and he tends to us as a good Father.

Don't give up hope today. Even on your darkest days, God has sustained you. However disheartened you have been, you can trust that he is not finished working in your life. Each day he offers you abundant grace and unending mercy. There isn't a need he cannot fill or a path he cannot make straight. He has everything you need, and he is delighted to share it with you.

Merciful Father, thank you for the hope I have in you. I trust you to continue moving in my life. When I am discouraged, help me remember your faithfulness.

On Your Side

Yahweh is my revelation-light
and the source of my salvation.
I fear no one!
I'll never turn back and run, for you, Yahweh,
surround and protect me.

PSALM 27:1 TPT

We have nothing to be afraid of because God is always with us. The glory of his presence transforms our hearts and lives. He has promised that he will surround and protect each of his children. This is life changing if we allow it to be. There is no trial, conflict, or anxiety that is too big for God to handle. His protection doesn't come with contingencies or limits. He is big enough, strong enough, and fully willing to walk alongside each of his children.

What would it look like to stand in confident assurance of God's goodness today? If you knew that God was for you, how would it change the way you move through your day? Perhaps you would worry less about the future, or you might feel stronger in the midst of trials. Grasp ahold of the truth found in Scripture and refuse to let it go. Stay steady in your belief that God is for you, and he is not against you.

Lord, shine on me and bless me with your presence today. Thank you for being on my side. I would be lost without your protection and guidance.

Precious to Him

"Since you were precious in My sight,
You have been honored,
And I have loved you;
Therefore I will give men for you,
And people for your life."

Isaiah 43:4 NKJV

We were created for connection and community. Sometimes we may struggle to fit in, or we may feel the need to shape-shift to fit the expectations of others. Thankfully, we never need to do that with our Maker. He knows each of us through and through. He wants us to experience wholeness and confidence in who he has created us to be. We can trust him and expect to find an innate sense of belonging in his presence.

You are not an afterthought to the Lord. You are precious, and you are wanted. You are fully seen, intimately known, and carefully loved. Don't resist God's delight in you. He wants you to know the power of his liberating love. He wants you to be free from doubt, shame, and fear. He wants you to know his affection as you reside in his presence.

God, I struggle to know the depths of your affection for me. Help me focus on how you see me instead of getting caught up in my own ideas. I trust your perspective over mine. Thank you for your kind love.

Test It Out

Examine and see how good the LORD is.
Happy is the person who trusts him.

PSALM 34:8 NCV

We are told to examine how good the Lord is. We have permission and freedom to test it out. God doesn't expect us to blindly believe what he says. His words are always backed up by actions. As such, if we look for his goodness, we will find it. We can see examples throughout Scripture, and we can hear testimonies of his goodness from people around us. God knows that if we examine his goodness we will return with assurance and confidence in his Word.

God has proven time and again that he is good, and he invites you to examine it. Look for his goodness and take note of it. Be deliberate in your search. God is not worried about what you will find. He doesn't have anything to hide. If you ask him to reassure you of his goodness, he will eagerly do it. Set your eyes on him, and you will not be disappointed.

Good Father, I want to see the goodness of your love in the details of my life. Help me see where you are already moving. Show me your heart and draw me closer to you.

Let Him Guide

I always let the LORD guide me.
Because he is at my right hand,
I will not be shaken.

PSALM 16:8 CSB

When we trust God's guidance, we can be sure he will lead us in the fullness of his love. There is no wilderness too dense for him, and there is no darkness he cannot light up. He is our constant companion and wise helper. We don't have to rely on our limited knowledge in any situation. He will help us, and he will continue to teach us with wisdom and patience. We can trust him and confidently follow his leadership because he knows what is best, and he will not lead us astray.

How do you typically make decisions? What factors influence your choices, and how do you navigate new situations? Remember that God is on your side. He is a better resource than anything you can find online. His wisdom is better than your intuition, and his guidance is more reliable than your best friend's. If you ask, he will faithfully guide you and direct your steps.

God, give me the confidence that comes from relying on you. I want to value your wisdom above all else. Thank you for guiding me and keeping me steady. I trust that you will keep me on the right path.

In Due Time

"There is nothing concealed that will not be disclosed,
or hidden that will not be made known."

LUKE 12:2 NIV

There are no hidden motives with God. He sees into
every heart, and he knows the lies that people weave. There
are a few scenarios where it's important to remember this
fact. We must realize that it isn't our responsibility to discern
what everyone's secrets are. We must also realize that we
ourselves cannot have secrets from God. The truth will
always come out, and in the end nothing will remain hidden.

God's ability to see everything should not make you
cower in fear. The fact that he knows the depths of your
heart should draw you closer to him. His omniscience is
fully combined with his eternal goodness and his unending
kindness. You have nothing to fear and nothing to hide
from the One who loves you without limits. You can rest in
God's faithfulness, and you can trust that his light will reveal
everything perfectly.

*God of truth, I cannot know or see everything perfectly. You
are the only one who sees the depths of my heart. Help me
embrace humility and continually lean on you.*

JULY

He brought me out
into a spacious place;
he rescued me
because he delighted in me.

PSALM 18:18 NIV

Walk by Faith

We walk by faith, not by sight.

2 Corinthians 5:7 ESV

Walking by faith means we understand this short life is not all that matters. We move through our days knowing we are connected to a much larger story. We don't make decisions based on our own understanding. Instead, we seek the Lord for wisdom and trust that his perspective is perfect, complete, and so much more expansive than ours.

You cannot see God, but you can experience his powerful presence. You don't yet know him fully, but you can follow the Holy Spirit as he points you to the Father. Though you are limited by the constraints of this lifetime, you have the assurance that one day you will experience the perfection of creation as God originally intended it to be. Be confident in the fact that your faith will not go unrewarded. A day is coming when everything will be perfectly seen and understood.

God, I want to walk by faith my whole life long. I choose to follow you even when the path is unclear. I trust you to lead me.

Ruled by Peace

Let the peace that comes from Christ rule in your hearts.
For as members of one body you are called to live in peace.
And always be thankful.

COLOSSIANS 3:15 NLT

It is natural to feel fear, but we don't have to let it rule us. As followers of Jesus, we have the privilege of giving him our fears. We can cast our cares upon him trusting that he will carry them. In exchange he gives us peace. The peace of Christ brings clarity of mind, quietness of heart, and the freedom needed to continue stepping out in faith.

It's easy to get lost in fear. Have you ever been so focused on your anxieties that you completely forget you can ask for help? You are not meant to be ruled by every whim or thought that passes through your mind. You are meant to be ruled by peace that comes from Christ. Remember that you can ask for his help in every situation, no matter how trivial it may seem. If it matters to you, it matters to God. Don't hesitate to invite him into your jumbled thoughts. He will faithfully lead you into a place of clarity and peace.

Powerful God, thank you for the peace of your presence. When I am overwhelmed, remind me to cast my fears upon you. May your perfect peace rule in my heart today.

Strength and Song

The Lord is my strength and song,
And He has become my salvation;
This is my God, and I will praise Him;
My father's God, and I will exalt Him.

Exodus 15:2 nasb

God is the same yesterday, today, and forever. He faithfully led his people out of captivity in Egypt, and he leads us today. He raised Jesus from the dead, and he offers us new life today. His power has not diminished or weakened. His ability to rescue his people has not changed. He is, and always has been, worthy of all our praise. He deserved to be worshipped when he led the Israelites through the desert, and he deserves to be worshipped in the middle of your most mundane day.

God is worthy of your praise in every season. When you witness miracles or pick up your groceries, praise God. When you weep at his feet or walk through the woods, praise God. In every situation, he is your strength and your song. Lift him high and exalt his name. As you turn to him in worship, he will revive your heart and draw you closer to himself.

God, I have tasted and seen your goodness. You have done great and mighty things for us. Draw me closer as I worship you. Thank you for all you've done.

Innate Worth

From now on, we refuse to evaluate people merely by their outward appearances. For that's how we once viewed the Anointed One, but no longer do we see him with limited human insight.

2 CORINTHIANS 5:16 TPT

It's not right to ascribe value to others based on their appearance. God does not accept us because of the style of our clothes or how put-together we seem to be. Our worth stems from the fact that we are his creation, and he is well pleased with us. Our very existence glorifies him. God loves each of us abundantly. His love is without limits or qualifying factors. When we equate appearance with worth, we put unnecessary limits on God's love.

In a culture that is so focused on outward appearance, it can be easy to fall into the habit of judging others. You aren't alone if you struggle in this area. It takes intentionality and discipline to see others without bias. Following Jesus means you humbly accept the undeserved mercy he offers each of his children. You can rest confidently in his great love, and you can generously share it with others.

Great God, thank you for the power of your limitless love. I want to see others the way you see them. I am so grateful that you look at my heart and not my outward appearance.

Trust and Wait

Lord, show your love to us
as we put our hope in you.

PSALM 33:22 NCV

Hope is an active trait. It combines trust with waiting. It believes in the best and refuses to give up. Today's verse reminds us that love and hope go hand-in-hand. We put our hope in God, and he responds but showing us his love. We trust that he has everything under control and will faithfully fulfill his promises. As we wait for him, we have the privilege of experiencing his perfect love. We don't wait empty-handed.

Put your hope in the Lord. He will not let you down. When everything around you feels unstable, you can trust that he will never fail. Everything he has said will come to pass. When your hope is in him, you won't waver when trials come. You won't be derailed by difficult circumstances. Hope keeps you steady no matter what storms you walk through. As you put your hope in God, let his love surround you and fill your heart.

God, please give me reassurance that you will fulfill your promises. I put my hope in you today. Fill me with your love as I wait for you. Thank you for not leaving me empty handed.

ABOVE IT ALL

Set your mind on things above,
not on things on the earth.

COLOSSIANS 3:2 NKJV

We are surrounded by distractions. It makes sense that many would be overcome by fear of the future. It's becoming increasingly less common to encounter people who are steady, confident, and unworried. The vast majority seem distraught about the state of the world. Everywhere we turn there is outrage, despair, and disagreements.

It's not wrong to be culturally aware. However, problems arise if you are consumed by the circumstances around you. You are not meant to find your security in economic, political, environmental, or social trends. As heirs to God's kingdom, you are called to set your mind on things above. It might take mental discipline, but your thoughts should be directed toward what is eternal. God's wealth will never deplete. His government will never fall. His creation will never decay, and the body of Christ will live forever.

King Jesus, I want to follow your ways and not the ways of this world. Align my thoughts with yours. Comfort me when I am distraught and draw my attention toward you.

He Can

Jesus said to him, "'If you can?'
Everything is possible for the one who believes."

MARK 9:23 CSB

A desperate father brought his son to Jesus and asked if he could heal him. Jesus responded by reassuring the man that he was fully capable of doing it. The father didn't need to use the word *if* when asking for help. There is no question as to whether or not Jesus can do what we ask. When we pray, do our requests insinuate that maybe Jesus can't accomplish what we need?

Today, ask God to give you a greater understanding of his power. If your prayers come with a caveat, ask yourself the reason. Do you doubt that God can move in your life? Do you assume he won't show up? Let God meet you in your weakness and doubt. He will respond to you with gentleness and kindness. Ask him to strengthen your faith, and he will. Ask him to remove your misconceptions, and he will.

Jesus, strengthen my faith today! Help me believe in the fullness of your power. I don't want to doubt you or limit what you can do. I give you my needs and I trust that you can take care of them.

Press On

I do not consider myself yet to have taken hold of it. But one
thing I do: Forgetting what is behind and straining toward
what is ahead, I press on toward the goal to win the prize for
which God has called me heavenward in Christ Jesus.

PHILIPPIANS 3:13-14 NIV

We are all on a journey in this life. It is not always a
linear path, and it doesn't typically look how we think it will.
Our lives often take turns we don't anticipate and end up in
places we never dreamed of. No matter how well we plan,
there's no way we can predict every situation we'll encounter.
This is why it is good to maintain the mindset found in
today's Scripture. Despite our differing circumstances, we
can all press on toward the same goal.

It can be easy to feel derailed by trials or circumstances
that aren't ideal. Instead of getting bogged down by what you
cannot control, lift your eyes, and stay focused on where you
are going. There is a day of perfection coming, and you need
only to persevere. Even your best day cannot compare to the
goodness that God has in store for you. Look forward with
eager anticipation and don't let today's worries cloud your
perspective.

*God, I want to follow you with endurance. Help me stay
focused on what is coming rather than being discouraged by
my current circumstances.*

PLANS MADE

"What no eye has seen, nor ear heard,
nor the heart of man imagined,
what God has prepared for those who love him."

1 CORINTHIANS 2:9 ESV

God is gracious and kind toward each of us. He desires to give good gifts that teach us about his unending love. His love is both broad and specific. He envelops all of creation in adoration, yet he also loves each of us in a way that is specific and catered to who we are. He makes plans for us that take our strengths, weaknesses, and personality into account. He is a good Father who teaches, guides, and protects his children.

God cares for you fully and completely. The perfection he has in store for you is better than anything you can imagine. Today, revel in his affection toward you. Close your eyes, take a deep breath, and imagine an existence that is completely free of conflict, trials, and pain. This is what he has prepared for you. This is what you have to look forward to. Let the promise of what's to come give you the strength you need to face whatever comes your way.

Faithful Father, thank you for your guidance and help every single day. I trust you with my future and my present. I surrender to you, for I know your plans are good!

WAIT AND TRUST

Let all that I am wait quietly before God,
for my hope is in him.

PSALM 62:5 NLT

Psalm 62 is an invitation and a lament. It is a stance of unshakable faith in the face of betrayal. It is a declaration of God's faithfulness despite the circumstances in the life of the author, David. When we are having a difficult day, this psalm can serve as our own declaration of faith. We can stand before our loving God and quietly surrendering to him. We can intentionally make room to wait patiently before God. As we trust and listen, he will surely speak.

When you are overwhelmed by life, you can position your heart before God and wait expectantly for him to meet you with the power of his presence. There will be days that challenge your sense of peace. There will be circumstances that distract you from faith in God. In those moments, no matter how far you've strayed, you can come before God and rest in his presence.

Mighty God, I wait quietly before you now. I turn my attention toward your voice and welcome you to move in my life! Speak, Lord. I am listening.

RESTORED AND SUSTAINED

Restore to me the joy of Your salvation,
And sustain me with a willing spirit.

PSALM 51:12 NASB

God is worthy of our trust in every moment. He never changes, and he is faithful through every season. God delights in restoring our hope, joy, and passion. He brings breakthroughs to the areas where we have been stuck. He sustains us, and he protects us when we aren't even aware of our need for it. All glory belongs to him, and he is worthy of all our praise.

Try to remember a time when you experienced God's faithfulness. The same loving Father is still with you, and he is working on your behalf. He has not abandoned you. He will never forsake you. You are free to wait patiently, follow wisely, and trust fully! He will restore the joy of your salvation once again. He is faithful and true, and you can always count on him. May you experience the grace and peace of his presence. May you always have the courage and confidence to lean on him for all you need.

God, I long for you to move on my behalf. You have done good things in my life, and you will keep sustaining me. Remind me of your faithful love and help me trust you while I wait.

Strong Roots

"Blessed are those who trust in the LORD
and have made the LORD their hope and confidence.
They are like trees planted along a riverbank,
with roots that reach deep into the water."

JEREMIAH 17:7-8 NLT

When you put your trust in the Lord, you root yourself in the soil of his faithful love. The result is that you will be nourished no matter what your circumstances are. You won't be ruined by droughts or storms because you are firmly planted in exactly the right spot. You will yield the fruit of the Spirit through every season. When hard times come, you will have God's light pouring over you.

What are the roots of your life established in? The rocky soil of self-sufficiency will only get you so far. The deficient soil of power and prestige won't feed your soul. There is so much life available to you through fellowship with your Maker. You can trust him today for everything you need. He offers you the resources of his kingdom, and he is delighted when you ask him for help!

Lord, I put my wholehearted trust in you. You remain the same through every battle and every season. Enrich my heart with the nourishment of your love today!

The Same Story

"Listen, Jacob, to the One who created you,
Israel, to the one who shaped who you are.
Do not fear,
for I, your Kinsman-Redeemer, will rescue you.
I have called you by name, and you are mine."

ISAIAH 43:1 TPT

In Christ, we have been adopted into God's family. If we are God's children, we can take his promises to heart! We can read his declarations to Israel and glean from them. If God rescued Israel, he will rescue us. We can look at what he has done in the past and be encouraged that he will do it again. His devotion to Israel and his pursuit of their freedom should strengthen our faith and cause us to worship.

God never changes. His character doesn't shift, and he doesn't alter his plans. The same God who redeemed Israel will redeem you. You are part of the same story. One day, all who have been rescued by God will rejoice together. You will worship him alongside those who walked through the parted sea. You will enjoy the delight of his presence alongside those who read Isaiah when it was written. Let this revelation spark a sense of purpose and belonging in your soul.

Creator, thank you for calling me into your family. I am blessed to be part of your story. Encourage me with your faithfulness and bless me with your presence.

Great Things

We were filled with laughter,
and we sang happy songs.
Then the other nations said,
"The Lord has done great things for them."
The Lord has done great things for us,
and we are very glad.

PSALM 126:2-3 NCV

When our long-awaited hope appears in the flesh,
we will be filled with joy! Christ's return will be like the
fulfillment of a dream that has been carried for a long time.
We will experience the fullness of his presence and the
delight of eternal salvation. Just as a marathon runner is
elated at the finish line, we will be overjoyed when we realize
the trials of this life are over.

Even when all hope seems lost, you don't have to doubt
what God has promised. Nothing can get in the way of his
plans. What he ordains will surely come to pass. No matter
how dark the night seems, dawn will appear at just the right
time. There may be circumstances in your life that seem
impossible. While you may not see a way out, God sees the
entire situation perfectly. Trust that he is capable of fulfilling
his promise of redemption. He will do great things for you.

*Redeemer, you are the God who brings restoration when hope
seems lost. I rejoice in your faithfulness.*

Free Indeed

The law of the Spirit of life in Christ Jesus has set you free
from the law of sin and death.

ROMANS 8:2 CSB

We are not bound by the law of sin and death. We
gained eternal freedom the moment we chose to put our
faith in Christ's work on the cross. There is no condemnation
when we make mistakes, and there is no judgment of our
past failures. God does not hold us accountable for things he
has already forgiven. This does not mean that we escape the
natural consequences of our actions. It means guilt no longer
rules over us, and our sin no longer separates us from God.

God sent his Son to release you from the law of sin
and death. He did this because he longs for you to be in his
presence. He loves you, and he wants you to spend eternity
with him just as he intended from the very beginning.
Through Christ he has made a way for you to live in
freedom. Instead of carrying the weight of your sin, you get
to know his joy, peace, and everlasting fellowship!

*Lord Jesus, you are my Savior and my hope. It is not always
easy to release myself from the guilt I feel when I make
mistakes. Set me free, and help me live according to your love,
grace, peace, and wisdom.*

Soul Satisfaction

Jesus answered, "I am the way and the truth and the life.
No one comes to the Father except through me."

JOHN 14:6 NIV

From the depths of our souls, we long to know the
Creator. We know deep inside that we have a greater purpose
than what our culture preaches. We can't ignore that eternity
calls to us, and we know we were meant for more than the
world offers. This longing is meant to draw us closer to God.
We are supposed to know him intimately. If we want to
know God, Jesus is our only path. His death and resurrection
are our open door to communion with our Maker.

There's a wide variety of belief systems in the world.
Most of them advocate for a higher meaning and some sort
of eternal fulfillment. You know that soul satisfaction comes
only from knowing Jesus. He is the way, the truth, and the
life. Any other path will lead you astray. Many will claim
they have solutions to your longing, but Jesus alone can lead
you to the Father.

Jesus, you are the way, the truth, and the life. When I am
tempted to find fulfillment in other ways, draw me back to
you. Hold me close and keep me steadily on your path of life.

Better Hope

On the one hand, a former commandment is set aside
because of its weakness and uselessness (for the law made
nothing perfect); but on the other hand, a better hope is
introduced, through which we draw near to God.

HEBREWS 7:18-19 ESV

Rigid rules can hold us back if they are based in a
tradition which keeps us small and stuck, rather than leading
us into the liberty of God's love. Christ set us free. We have
the freedom to choose how we live, and we don't have to
stay stuck in patterns that no longer serve our growth or our
health. We are given the greater option to draw near to God
and follow his path. It doesn't always look how we expect,
but it does always lead to the fullness of love, life, and peace.

For people who like lists and a clear sense of
accomplishment, the law might actually sound appealing. If
you fall into that category, you'll need to guard your heart.
While rules and lists seem safe and easy to understand, they
don't lead to the freedom that God desires for you. Be wary
of your own tendency to elevate your achievements above
the mercy that has been generously bestowed upon you.
Christ is your better hope. What he achieved on the cross
will outlast even your greatest successes.

*Lord, you are always the better hope. I don't want to be a slave
to the law. I choose to follow you, even when it goes against
my comfort or my preferences.*

Adopted

God decided in advance to adopt us into his own family by bringing us to himself through Jesus Christ. This is what he wanted to do, and it gave him great pleasure.

EPHESIANS 1:5 NLT

When a child is adopted, they don't have to prove themselves worthy of adoption. There is no process in which they have to convince someone that they are good enough to be included in their family. The new parents have the authority to make a distinct and willful decision to adopt. Out of love, they welcome the child into their home and decide that they are part of their family. Beloved, it is the same for us in God's family. All of the authority is on God's side of the equation. We don't have to prove our worthiness.

It gave God great pleasure to make you a part of his family. You have a seat at his table simply because he wants you there. He is delighted by your presence, and he is happy that you can be near to him. Out of his great love for you, he made a way for you to spend eternity in his family. His love for you will not waver, and your position as his heir cannot be shaken.

Father, I'm grateful for your devoted love which makes me yours. I don't want to live at a distance from you. Bring me close to you and teach me your ways. I am so glad to be your child!

No More Shame

Now the case is closed. There remains no accusing voice of
condemnation against those who are joined in life-union
with Jesus, the Anointed One.

ROMANS 8:1 TPT

The voice of condemnation is sharp and accusatory. It
is fault-finding and relentless. It looks for flaws to nitpick
and for ways to increase shame. Condemnation tells us that
we aren't good enough and that we never will be. Its voice
is harsh, demeaning, and cruel. This is never the voice of
our heavenly Father. God's correction is always loving. His
kindness, not his accusation, leads us to repentance.

If you think about your life, has there ever been a time
when negativity and shame brought about positive change?
The answer is likely no. You can't make lasting change when
you feel belittled and unsupported. God's love empowers
you and lifts you up. He holds your weaknesses tenderly and
gives you grace to move out of sin and into freedom. God's
gentle voice is easy to surrender to. You can trust him with
every part of you, no matter how dark or broken, because he
will always have mercy on you.

*Lord, you have set me free from my sin. Help me continually
surrender to you instead of carrying the weight of shame.
Silence the voice of condemnation and lead me in your love!*

RELATIONSHIP FIRST

"I desire loyalty rather than sacrifice,
And the knowledge of God rather than burnt offerings."

HOSEA 6:6 NASB

In the Old Testament, people made sacrifices to atone for their sins. It was required under the law of Moses to make reparation for your mistakes and failures. When God stated today's verse in Hosea, he redirected the focus of his requirements from outer actions to the inner issues of the heart. This has always been what he wanted. God has always valued relationships over religious requirements.

It is good to evaluate the traditions you uphold. Take time to check your heart and ensure you aren't elevating your own actions above God's mercy. It's easy to become bound to habits and rituals rather than trusting God has done the work for you. He cares less about what you do and more about what's happening in your heart. Remember that true fellowship with him matters more than how good you are at following rules.

Lord God, I don't want to go through the motions without knowing you. May I experience your presence today and know you in ways I have not yet experienced.

Pursued by Goodness

Why would I fear the future?
Only goodness and tender love
pursue me all the days of my life.
Then afterward, when my life is through,
I'll return to your glorious presence to be forever with you!

PSALM 23:6 TPT

The goodness that pursues us is not about riches, fame, or worldly success. It is about God himself. He pursues us with a passion that is undeterred. He can take our biggest disappointments and create a garden of glory from the rubble. He is the God of redemption, restoration, and second chances. As long as we are living, the goodness of his presence is pursuing us.

Do you fear the future? Is there something inside of you that is waiting for the other shoe to drop? Perhaps you have experienced hardship and are struggling to see any goodness in the situation. Maybe the difficulties in your life are beginning to diminish your hope. Even when things don't look the way you want, you can rely on God's promises. You can look beyond your perception of your experiences and trust that if God says goodness will follow you, it will.

God, open my eyes to see where you have relentlessly pursued me with goodness and tender love. Your faithfulness is not dependent on my understanding. You are so kind and faithful!

Trust in Him

The Lord is good,
A stronghold in the day of trouble;
And He knows those who trust in Him.

NAHUM 1:7 NKJV

No matter what trouble we find ourselves in, the Lord remains faithful and good. He will not withhold help from us when we ask him. We can give him our heaviest concerns and our smallest worries. He can handle them all! No problem is too big for him to handle, and no care is so small that it is insignificant to him. He lovingly and perfectly cares for each of us.

Take heart, beloved! You can trust God with whatever weighs on you. His love covers you, and his wisdom is available in every challenge you face. He will guide you through the most complicated path, and he will comfort you on your darkest days. Turn your worries over to him as many times as is necessary; he will never tire of your prayers. He doesn't want you to struggle through your days alone. He longs to be near you, encourage you, and equip you.

God, I have known your faithfulness before, and I trust that I will see it again. Help me rest in faith and allow you to do what only you can do. Relieve my fears and lift my burdens. I offer them to you today!

REAL LOVE

Your love must be real.
Hate what is evil, and hold on to what is good.

ROMANS 12:9 NCV

We live in a culture that elevates self-care. While we should certainly be aware of our health, it's worth it to ask if we are too focused on ourselves. Do we despise serving others and call it self-care? Real love requires sacrifice. If we are unsure of how to love others, we can look at Jesus' example. He laid his life down in humility. He didn't insist on his own way or hide to protect himself.

God cares for you. You are his beloved child, and he wants you to experience the depths of his love. He gives you everything you need. From that place of fulfillment, he asks you to care for others. He loves you to overflowing and then asks you to love others. Ask yourself if you are trusting God to care for you or if you are trying to handle it on your own. No amount of self-care will replace the goodness of God's presence. Soak up the abundant and real love he has for you and then offer it to those around you.

God, fill me with your love today. Refresh me as I spend time in your presence. I trust you to take care of me. Help me share your love with those around me.

The Good Way

You are good, and you do what is good;
teach me your statutes.

PSALM 119:68 CSB

Our ultimate model of goodness doesn't lie in a list of virtues. Our own perception of what is right isn't reliable. No matter how hard we try, our humanity inevitably gets in the way of our pursuit of perfection. Our ultimate example of goodness rests in God himself. His perfection is unmatched. He is the only standard we can use to measure ourselves.

When you compare yourself to God, you will surely fall short. There is no way that you can measure up. This is why the Gospel is such good news. Because of Jesus, your imperfections are no longer in the way. You have been set free and can now live the way God wants you to. In his goodness, he will faithfully teach you what is right. He loves to guide and instruct his children. If you let him, he will lead you on a path that honors him.

God, when I don't know what to do or how to move ahead, I look to you. I am so thankful you are my guide, my teacher, and my friend. I trust you to lead me in goodness.

Forgive Freely

Be kind and compassionate to one another, forgiving each
other, just as in Christ God forgave you.

EPHESIANS 4:32 NIV

Forgiveness is not always easy. In fact, the very need
for it indicates there has been a break in trust. There is a
wound in a relationship, and healing must be pursued. No
matter the severity of the wound, forgiveness is always the
way forward. It is the path of restoration. There cannot be
regained trust without repentance and forgiveness.

When you ask God to forgive you, he does it eagerly and
completely. He restores you to right standing before him, and
he embraces you with an all-encompassing love. While this
is your model for forgiveness, God is not surprised by the
way you might stumble through it. He knows your deepest
hurts, and he knows that you aren't naturally inclined to
forgive freely. This is why you must depend on his grace
and keep your heart soft toward his instruction. When your
desire is to seek restoration, no matter how hard it is, he will
lead you with gentleness.

Merciful Father, thank you for your liberating forgiveness.
Help me freely forgive others. When I struggle, give me grace,
and empower me to love like you do. Help me remain humble
and willing to restore what is broken.

WAIT WELL

Be strong, and let your heart take courage,
all you who wait for the LORD!

PSALM 31:24 ESV

Waiting is rarely easy; it's significantly harder when we don't have any idea how long we'll be waiting. Life rarely follows our own timelines, and the details of God's provision don't always look the way we think they should. No matter what our circumstances are, we can trust in God's faithfulness. He will come through. He will never leave or forsake his children. The more we trust that he will be true to his word, the more we can persevere through seasons of waiting.

What does it look like for your heart to take courage today? You may have a different answer to that question depending on the season of life you're in. Maybe you need encouragement in an area of life where you are struggling. Maybe you need strength to endure a drawn-out trial. Whatever your need is, you can have confidence that God will provide it. Even if it takes longer than you think it should, he will always fulfill his promises.

Lord, I need courage for my circumstances right now. I know you see every detail of my life, and you won't fail to provide what I need. As I trust in you, give me the confidence I need to wait patiently.

God's Smile

May the LORD smile on you
and be gracious to you.

NUMBERS 6:25 NLT

God is our place of respite. It's so easy to get caught up in the chaos of life that we forget to enjoy his presence. No matter what storms we face, God is with us. No matter how confusing, unexpected, or frustrating our circumstances are, God is faithful. We can be strengthened by his kindness and encouraged by his delight. He longs for his people to turn toward him.

Let God's blessing wash over you. Close your eyes and listen to his voice. It is calm, life-giving, and powerful. God desires good things for your life. Rest in his kindness and let his peace soothe your tired soul. You are held and eternally loved by your Maker. He keeps you, and he hems you in. He wants you to experience his affection and know that he is smiling over you. You are dear to him, and nothing can remove you from his hands.

God, I want to feel your smile over me. Help me slow down and enjoy your presence. You have been so faithful to me. Thank you for showering me with mercy and grace.

Be Nourished

Like newborn babies, long for the pure milk of the word,
so that by it you may grow in respect to salvation,
if you have tasted the kindness of the Lord.

1 Peter 2:2-3 nasb

The Word of God nourishes our souls so we can grow strong and remain faithful. When we experience God's kindness and goodness, it makes us hungry for more of him. That hunger can be satisfied by filling our hearts with the Word. We can read Scripture or listen to it while we drive. No matter how busy life seems, there is always time and space to value God's Word. It equips, encourages, and empowers us. Without the nourishment of the Word, we hinder our own growth.

There are no established standards for filling your life with the Word. Don't get caught up in rules or regulations. You don't have to read one chapter per day or memorize a certain amount. Instead of seeking to fulfill requirements, seek to satisfy your hunger. Ask the Holy Spirit to give you an affection for God's Word. You can be confident he will do it.

Lord, I want to grow in maturity. Fill me with a desire to know your Word. Give me understanding and discernment as I read. Teach me your ways and fill me with truth.

Respond Rightly

Make every effort to respond to God's promises. Supplement
your faith with a generous provision of moral excellence, and
moral excellence with knowledge, and knowledge with self-
control, and self-control with patient endurance, and patient
endurance with godliness, and godliness with brotherly
affection, and brotherly affection with love for everyone.

2 Peter 1:5-7 nlt

Jesus' sacrifice made a way for us to spend eternity
with God. We are redeemed and set free from the power of
sin and death. We have been given an abundance of grace
and God has poured mercy over our lives. All of this is
wildly undeserved and should stir our hearts toward greater
devotion. We are meant to respond to God's promises with a
life that is surrendered to his ways.

Your faith is not meant to be stagnant. Look at the
glorious things God has done for you and offer your life to
him in return. Acknowledge the grace you've been given and
humbly follow in Jesus's footsteps. Seek moral excellence,
knowledge, self-control, endurance, and love. These are the
things God desires to see in your life. You cannot earn the
grace you need, but you can respond to it.

*God, fill me with your Holy Spirit. I submit myself to you, and
I trust that you will graciously lead me.*

Great Kindness

Lord, answer me because your love is so good.
Because of your great kindness, turn to me.

Psalm 69:16 ncv

God is not cold or aloof. He does not lean down to hear your cries and then willfully ignore you. He is unfailingly merciful. He is always patient. He is attentive and kind. If we were convinced that God would answer our prayers today, what would we ask for? Would the way we interact with our loving Father be different if we truly understood his character?

With great kindness, God turns his attention toward you. He answers your cries, and he provides for your needs. You can be sure of his faithfulness! You can trust him to answer you, even if the answer is not what you imagined. His ways are best, and he will not withhold anything good from you. You can trust his timing and his kindness. He will not fail you!

God, I won't hold back my real requests from you today. I trust you to see what is in my heart. You know exactly what I need. Answer me with kindness and encourage me with your presence.

DESIRABLE TRAITS

What is desired in a man is kindness,
And a poor man is better than a liar.

PROVERBS 19:22 NKJV

God has laid out everything he requires of us in his own nature. What he asks for, he provides in his presence. He is a deep well of kindness and a strong foundation of truth. We are meant to reflect his character, and he helps us to do it every step of the way. Scripture is full of admonitions and instructions for living wisely. We honor God when we seek to live in a way that pleases him.

God honors your willing heart. If you want to grow in kindness and honesty, he will help you. He is delighted by your desire to reflect his character. He is gracious toward you and will help you grow. Don't be intimidated or ashamed of your current flaws. Your weaknesses allow God's strength to be magnified. Even so, he will patiently walk with you as you mature and grow.

God, thank you for your incomparable nature. I want to be transformed with your love! Walk with me as I grow in patience and kindness. Teach me how to be more like you.

August

The steadfast love of the LORD never ceases; his mercies never come to an end; they are new every morning; great is your faithfulness.

LAMENTATIONS 3:22-23 ESV

Unhindered

This hope is a strong and trustworhty anchor for our souls.
It leads us through the curtain into God's inner sanctuary.

HEBREWS 6:19 NLT

We were once impossibly separated from God. The only place that he could be seen was the inner sanctuary of the tabernacle. The priest was the only one who had access, and the process was bound up with meticulous rules and rituals. God's presence was restricted, and people needed the priest to meet with him on their behalf. Jesus is now our wonderful priest. Through him we have constant and unrestricted access to God's presence. His death and resurrection allowed us to walk past the curtain and into the inner sanctuary of God.

God has redeemed you to himself. He is no longer hidden from you. There is nothing standing between you and his glorious presence. When you feel as though you can't find him, remember that the curtain has been torn and you have full access. Push past how you feel and find confidence in what Jesus has done. Your feelings cannot change the truth; God is with you always. You don't ever have to be apart from him again.

God, I'm in awe of your glorious plan! Thank you for redeeming me. I'm so glad I can enter into your presence whenever I want. Fill my heart with your love and draw me close to your heart.

MISPLACED DESIRE

Yes, LORD, walking in the way of your laws,
we wait for you;
your name and renown
are the desire of our hearts.

ISAIAH 26:8 NIV

We were created to worship God alone. He made us in his image, and we belong with him. We are part of him. As such, his presence is the only place we will find satisfaction and fulfillment. If we look anywhere else, we will come up short. No matter how hard we try, there is nothing that will fill our souls like the love of God.

Have you ever interacted with a child in desperate need of a nap? They are unreasonable and often convinced they need everything but sleep. They'll beg for anything they can think of and will fight the heaviness of their eyelids until the very last moment. When you misplace your desire, you are like that sleepy child. You can adamantly throw yourself at other sources of satisfaction, but your soul will continue to long for what you really need. You were created to desire the renown of your heavenly Father. Only in him will you be truly satisfied.

King of Kings, I desire to know you more than anything else. I surrender my life to you. You are worthy of all my praise!

His Success

Not by their own sword did they win the land,
nor did their own arm save them,
but your right hand and your arm,
and the light of your face,
for you delighted in them.

PSALM 44:3 ESV

God's glorious power delivered the Israelites and brought them into the land of their inheritance. The same is true for us. We don't take our destinies by force. God opens the door for us to go in the direction he wants; he is the One who does it. Success in our lives is not a testament to our own skills but to his goodness and mercy. Every talent and strength we have is bestowed upon us by our generous Creator.

Is there something you've been fighting for but have not experienced the breakthrough you need? Perhaps it is time to stop striving and turn to the Lord. Instead of depending on your own abilities, ask him to move on your behalf. Remember that he is able and willing to help you. You can trust him to do what you cannot! Don't resist his guidance even when you don't understand the direction it takes.

Faithful God, I don't want to resist your leadership in my life because of my own ideas. I need you to move on my behalf. Help me faithfully follow you no matter where you lead me.

Faithfully Moving

The Lord is righteous in everything he does;
he is filled with kindness.

PSALM 145:17 NLT

God's loyal love can be seen in everything he does. He weaves threads of mercy through the patterns of our lives until we become beautiful tapestries of his redemption. The Holy Spirit opens the eyes of our hearts so we can see where God is working in the details of our lives. Sometimes we have to look closely at specific situations, and sometimes we have to zoom out a little to see the big picture. Either way, there is definitive evidence of God's goodness in the lives of his children.

When you struggle to see God's hand at work in your story, ask for a new perspective. Ask him to show you evidence of his mercy, and he will faithfully reveal it to you. God's work can be seen wherever you have seen kindness, grace, peace, restoration, or joy. Even the very breath in your lungs testifies of his provision in your life. There's no need to overcomplicate or over spiritualize what God has done for you. He has been faithful to you, and he will continue to be.

Lord, I know that you are good and do all things perfectly. Where there is doubt in my heart and mind, please bring clarity and confidence. Show me how you have been faithfully moving in my life.

Gratitude for Goodness

Give thanks to the Lord, for He is good;
For His faithfulness is everlasting.

1 Chronicles 16:34 nasb

God is good and his faithfulness is everlasting. Every act of goodness we experience or witness in someone else's life can be fuel for gratitude. When we recognize that all good things come from him, we open the door for constant praise. There is no shortage of reasons to worship the Lord. From the rising to the setting of the sun, creation is filled to overflowing with evidence of his goodness.

Today, take a few minutes to make a gratitude list. Don't overthink it. There is nothing so small that God doesn't deserve the praise for it. As you practice the discipline of thanksgiving, you may find that your eyes are opened to the expanse of God's goodness. You may begin to see him at work everywhere you look. As you notice his hand on your life, praise him and thank him for all he is doing.

God, thank you for your goodness. Help me see all the ways you are at work in my life. I don't want to be blind toward the work of your hands.

Great Confidence

"Behold—God is my salvation!
I am confident, unafraid, and I will trust in you."
Yes! The Lord Yah is my might and my melody;
he has become my salvation!

ISAIAH 12:2 TPT

Confidence is not to be confused with pride. There is a distinct difference between the two. Confidence is related to trust. Pride is related to self-satisfaction and an improper elevation of ourselves. Pride comes from thinking we are capable on our own. Confidence comes from realizing that God is the only one who can help us. Our desperate need for him, and his gracious response to us, gives us great confidence.

Society often elevates pride as a quality worth pursuing. You're told that it's good to elevate yourself and push for your opinions to be heard. Scripture reminds you that God is the one who should be lifted high. Place your trust in his ways and you won't be disappointed. When you feel pushed to make your voice heard, go against what's popular and lift God up instead. Pursue confidence in him over pride in yourself.

God, be magnified and lifted high in my life! When everyone around me is elevating themselves, I want to worship you. Be glorified by how I live. My confidence is in you.

IMAGE OF GOD

He is the image of the invisible God,
the firstborn over all creation.

COLOSSIANS 1:15 NKJV

Jesus Christ is the true likeness of God. No one has seen the Father, but we have seen Jesus. He walked the earth, interacted with people, and offered us a living picture of who the Father is. His life revealed the nature of God. Any questions we have about him can be answered by looking at Jesus. What a gift! After hundreds of years of waiting, God revealed himself to the world.

One day, Jesus will return, and you will live forever in fullness of God's presence. Until that day, you can be encouraged and learn from Christ's first coming. His life is an incredible gift. Be encouraged by his character and his actions. Look at how he loved, served, suffered, and endured. Everything he did reflected God. He is your perfect window into God's kingdom. Learn from the way Jesus walked the earth and let it draw you closer to the Father.

Lord Jesus, shine the light of your presence on me as I wait on you. Reveal the power of your love, the wisdom of your Word, and the freedom of your grace. Thank you for revealing the Father to the world.

Eyes to See

The LORD gives sight to the blind.
The LORD lifts up people who are in trouble.
The LORD loves those who do right.

PSALM 146:8 NCV

Jesus touched blind eyes and made them see. God's power can heal the physically blind and give them sight. Physical healing is incredible and a testimony of God's great ability, but it isn't the only way unseeing eyes can be opened. When we ask, the Holy Spirit opens the eyes of our hearts to understand the mysteries of God. He renews our perspective and aligns our thoughts with God's. He points us toward Scripture and teaches us how to think and move as Jesus did.

If you want to grow in understanding, ask God. He will faithfully open the eyes of your heart. He will not leave you blind and lost. He will give you insight and increase your knowledge. God loves to give good gifts. When you posture yourself before him in humility, he will meet you with generosity. Instead of using your limited perspective, lean on God's ability to see everything perfectly.

God of miracles, open my eyes to see your ways, to understand your nature, and to know the depths of your truth. I want to see as you see. Give me your perspective. Fill me today with wisdom and knowledge.

Reciprocal Love

"I love those who love me,
and those who search for me find me."

PROVERBS 8:17 CSB

Every time we pour our hearts out to the Lord, we are filled with his love. Everything we give to God has first been offered to us by him. Any amount of effort on our end is a response to what God has already done. He has pursued his people faithfully. We are the delight of his heart and his highest priority. Everything he does stems from the endless love he has for his creation.

There is nothing as powerful as a love that is reciprocated. When you give your heart and someone offers theirs in return, you are filled with delight, security, and joy! When you reach out to God, you can be convinced that he will reciprocate your effort. After all, he has generously reached out to you first. Every time you look toward him, you will be met with gracious and abundant love.

God, you are the object of my affection. I boldly offer you all I have, knowing there is so much more that I receive from you!

Met Beyond Measure

"Do not be afraid, little flock, for your Father has been
pleased to give you the kingdom."

LUKE 12:32 NIV

We easily worry about our necessities, getting caught
up in anxiety about what we will eat, drink, or wear. If we
seek the kingdom of God first, we don't have to worry about
the rest. He will care for us, for God is a faithful and good
Father. We are his flock, and he has declared that we will
inherit his entire kingdom. Our needs are beyond met.

When worry creeps into your thoughts, surrender it to
the Lord. Lay your anxiety at his feet and let him minister
to your heart. Don't let the hardships of this life pile up until
you can't step forward under their weight. Pass each burden
to your Father as soon as you encounter it. As you habitually
give him your worries, you will find that they lose their
power in your life.

*Father, I give you my fears and anxieties. You know exactly
what I am worried about. My needs are in your hands, and
I trust you to take care of me. Give me confidence in your
ability and fill my heart with peace.*

Heirs of Promise

If you are Christ's, then you are Abraham's offspring,
heirs according to promise.

GALATIANS 3:29 ESV

Many of us struggle with imposter syndrome. We may feel as if we don't belong in some way or that perhaps we are not qualified to fill the position we have. We focus on our flaws and insist that there is someone better for the job. The anxiety we feel does not usually reflect the reality of our situation. We may be incredibly successful but still not feel we deserve it.

In Christ, you have no reason to feel anxiety about your place in God's kingdom. Your position is secure because of what Christ did on the cross. You don't need to worry about your insufficiencies or what makes you inadequate. You are an heir to the promise along with all God's people. You can come with confidence to the throne of your heavenly Father, and you will be met with grace and mercy every time.

Abba, remind me of who I am in you. Speak truth over my soul and renew my mind with your wisdom. I am so thankful to be yours.

No Favorites

God does not show favoritism.

ROMANS 2:11 NLT

There will never be a shortage of God's love. It is vast enough to meet the needs of each person. There is no competition with God's love; we don't have to fight for his attention. We each have the audience of our good Father whenever we need him. God's love is expansive, and we are free to receive the depths of it.

When it comes to God's lack of favoritism, which side of the spectrum do you fall on? Do you elevate yourself and pridefully assume a position above others? Or do you demean yourself and sit under the weight of self-hatred and insecurity? Both scenarios take judgment out of God's hands and lift your opinion above his. Ask God to adjust your perspective. He will gently reveal his heart to you and fill you with his love.

Father, I want to experience the fullness of your love. Give me your perspective. Help me see myself and others the way you do.

RECONCILED

We also celebrate in God through our Lord Jesus Christ, through whom we have now received the reconciliation.

ROMANS 5:11 NASB

In Christ, we have been reconciled to God. Anything that once stood between us and God has been removed. There is nothing in the way of full fellowship with the Father. We have complete access to him in this renewed relationship. Where there was once a great impassable chasm, there is now unlimited joy and peace in the presence of God.

Think about a time when you had a big fight with someone you cared about. How did you feel when you weren't on good terms? Now consider how it felt when you reconciled with that person. Though the process of restoration can be difficult and create feelings of vulnerability, the end result is beautiful. Christ has done all the hard work of reconciling us to the Father. We only need to come to him in order to enter into fellowship with God. What a gracious gift!

Gracious Jesus, thank you for reconciling humanity with God. I am in awe of your love. I praise you for all you've done. May my life honor your sacrifice.

Amazing Grace

Even when we were dead and doomed in our many sins, he united us into the very life of Christ and saved us by his wonderful grace!

EPHESIANS 2:5 TPT

God's grace is so generous! It doesn't matter what we've done; his grace offers us a fresh start each morning. He removes every stain and every ounce of guilt with his perfect love! When we surrender our hearts to him, there is nothing but freedom waiting for us. There is no accusation or shame in the presence of God. There is no outstanding debt or list of requirements we must meet. The liberation of our souls is complete and final!

When you are at your worst, God's love is present and powerful. Be wary of rejecting God's grace by trying to earn a place in his kingdom on your own. Your position has already been secured. There is nothing you can do to get a better seat at the table. You can confidently stand before God, fully redeemed, and restored.

Gracious God, thank you for the free gift of salvation! I don't have to earn it or work to maintain it. Lead me into the fullness of life with you. May my actions reflect the mercy you've so graciously given me.

Mercy Triumphs

Judgment is without mercy to the one who has shown
no mercy. Mercy triumphs over judgment.

JAMES 2:13 NKJV

When we follow the law of love, we let go of the right
to judge others. Judgment belongs to God, for he sees
everything perfectly. He has clarity that we don't have, and
he knows every heart and motivation. We are asked to give
up harsh criticism and choose mercy instead. It is only
right to display mercy for others when God has been so
extravagantly merciful to us.

It's easy to cling to justice and judgment when you
forget your own humanity. Depending on the details of your
testimony, you may not have examples in your own life of
being pulled from the wreckage of sin onto the steady rock
of salvation. Maybe you turned to God at a young age, or
maybe you simply don't have propensities toward certain
sins. Either way, it's important to realize that you have
received the same amount of mercy as anyone else. When
you grasp how undeserving you are, you can display God's
mercy to others without judgment.

*Merciful God, help me depend on your judgment over my
own. Give me a revelation of the mercy I've received so I can
be merciful toward others. Keep me from letting incorrect
judgments get in the way of loving those around me.*

Sacred Secrets

"Judah, pray to me, and I will answer you. I will tell you
important secrets you have never heard before."

JEREMIAH 33:3 NCV

If we pray to God, he will answer us. He loves to
communicate with his children, and he is delighted by our
desire to hear from him. He is full of wisdom, and he wants
to be involved in our lives. When we look at him, he gives us
clarity instead of confusion and guidance where we need it.
He does not stay hidden from those who seek him. He readily
reveals himself, and he shares all that he has with his children.

Approach God with confidence knowing that he is
happy to reveal his heart to you. He will share who he is
and how much he loves you. God will never direct you
to do something that is outside of his character. He won't
reveal something to you that doesn't line up with Scripture.
Everything he says or does is good and right. God offers
peace for troubled hearts, vision for clouded eyes, strength
for feeble knees, and perseverance for the weary. As you
trust and pray, God answers.

Heavenly Father, thank you for answering me when I pray!
More than anything else, I want to hear your voice. Soften my
heart and give me ears to hear what you have to say.

Let God

Righteousness and justice are the foundation
of your throne;
faithful love and truth go before you.

PSALM 89:14 CSB

Everything God does is from a posture of loyal love and uncompromising truth. Righteousness and justice are the foundations of his throne. No one on earth is as just as God. Every decision he makes is full of wisdom. He takes every detail into account, and he doesn't miss a single factor. He sees every situation clearly, and his judgments are always perfect.

Have you ever been in a conflict and felt like the other person just didn't understand? Maybe you frantically tried to explain your position, or maybe you let bitterness grow in your heart when you realized they couldn't or wouldn't see your perspective. It's easy to get tangled in emotions and misjudge a situation. This never happens to God. When justice is your priority, seek the Lord. Place your desire for rightness into his hands and let him handle the situation. Release your burdens and let his perfect justice reign.

Lord, take my desire for justice and vindication. Your ways are perfect, and I cannot judge like you can. Soften my heart and help me trust you. Ground me in your gracious love and flood my heart with your understanding and compassion.

Follow the Shepherd

"My sheep listen to my voice;
I know them, and they follow me."

JOHN 10:27 NIV

Psalm 23 describes what a good shepherd is like. He provides all we need. He leads us into refreshing rest. He directs us through dark valleys, and he protects us along the way. Jesus Christ is our Shepherd. He provides for us, guides us, and protects us. He is faithful and trustworthy. He cares for us even when we wander.

You can trust Jesus to care for you and to bring you into the light of his kingdom. When you hear him, you can follow him without hesitation. He is trustworthy, and his instructions are for your benefit. Turn your attention toward him and trust that he will speak to you. No one will ever care for you like Jesus. He knows you better than you know yourself, and he only wants what is best for you.

Good Shepherd, guide me today. You know what I need better than I do. I willingly submit to your leadership. Help me hear your voice.

BITTER INTO SWEET

He cried to the LORD, and the LORD showed him a log,
and he threw it into the water, and the water became sweet.

EXODUS 15:25 ESV

God made bitter water drinkable when Moses cried out
on Israel's behalf. He turned the bitter into sweet. God also
does this in our lives. There are some things we come up
against that seem hopeless and impossible; we cannot see
any good in them at all. Only God is capable of turning our
worst situations into something that glorifies him and works
for our good. When we cry out to him, we should expect
that he will do what only he can do.

God loves to move in your life. He does not expect you
to follow him while he ignores you. He wants to hear from
you, and he wants to be intricately involved in your daily
routines. Let him take what is bitter and make it sweet. You
might be surprised by the impossible things he does in your
life. Be blessed by his presence and let him heal parts of your
heart you've forgotten about or given up on.

*Lord, I cry out for you for help. Take the bitter parts of my life
and make them sweet. Do what only you can do and bring
hope to the tired parts of my heart!*

God's Promises

Since there was no one greater to swear by,
God took an oath in his own name, saying:
"I will certainly bless you,
and I will multiply your descendants beyond number."

HEBREWS 6:13-14 NLT

God's promise to Abraham was based on the integrity of his own character. It was not based upon Abraham's performance. God did not remove the promise when Hagar gave birth to Ishmael. Even though Abraham deviated from his plan, he faithfully followed through on his vow. Abraham and Sarah had a son late in life and against all odds.

When God makes a promise, you don't have to make it happen. He takes full responsibility for his word, and he will do what it takes to fulfill it. You may look at your mistakes and think you've lost our chance, but that's not how God's faithfulness works. It is dependent on his nature, not yours. What a glorious relief this is! What God does, he does well. His plans are better than you can hope for, beyond your comprehension, and always defined by mercy.

Faithful God, I'm so glad your faithfulness doesn't depend on me. Give me grace to stop striving and lean fully on you. Help me overcome my internal fight for perfection.

WONDERFUL TESTIMONIES

Sing to the LORD, all the earth;
Proclaim good news of His salvation from day to day.
Tell of His glory among the nations,
His wonderful deeds among all the peoples.

1 CHRONICLES 16:23-24 NASB

It is encouraging to hear how God faithfully meets the needs of the people around us. Even when we don't directly benefit from a blessing, our faith is strengthened when we see evidence of God's ability to provide for his children. Whether it's good news after a doctor's appointment or provision for an outstanding bill, the benefits of God's faithfulness spread to all who witness it. Sometimes we need to look beyond our own lives and see that God is moving.

If you need a reason to sing to the Lord today, look for testimonies of his faithfulness from those around you. Ask others how God has provided for them and be encouraged by the answers. In the same way, don't be shy when it comes to sharing how God has shown up in your own life. Rejoice over the things he's done and let the body of Christ be lifted up by your testimony.

Lord, I know that you are working all around me in marvelous ways. May I be an encouragement to others and may the testimonies of your people strengthen me.

MADE NEW

The One who was sitting on the throne said, "Look! I am
making everything new!" Then he said, "Write this, because
these words are true and can be trusted."

REVELATION 21:5 NCV

God's plan is full of redemption, restoration, and
new life. He loves to sow mercy into the soil of our lives
and watch as new life springs up in due time. There isn't
a disappointment or loss from which God can't bring
goodness! One day, when our perspectives are no longer
limited, we will see the fruit of God's faithful love in every
detail of our lives.

Is there something in your life that needs to be made
new? Run to Jesus, the author and perfecter of your faith. He
will bring new life to areas you thought were long dead. Each
time he does this in your life it is foreshadowing of the way
he will renew the whole earth when he comes back. Each
glimpse of redemption speaks to the bigger story of how he
will restore all things to the way they were meant to be. You
will not be disappointed by Christ's ability to make all things
new, both now and for eternity.

*Perfect One, thank you for being a God who restores. I trust
your faithful love to come through when I need it most. Bring
new life to the areas of my heart that are tired and broken.*

Songs of Redemption

My lips shall greatly rejoice when I sing to You,
And my soul, which You have redeemed.

PSALM 71:23 NKJV

Whenever we come before the throne of God, we are met with overwhelming mercy. His love covers our mistakes. He gives us grace to start over whenever we need to. May the songs we offer God come from the depths of our love and gratitude for all he has done. May our worship come from a place of thankfulness and humility. He is delighted by the praise we offer to him.

The praise you offer to God is not limited to corporate worship. Sunday morning is not the only time you can engage in worship. Your entire life can be a fragrant offering to the Lord. Each day let praise flow from your lips. Rejoice in the little blessings you see and thank him for the miracles you experience. The more you walk in thanksgiving, the more natural it becomes.

God, I offer my praise to you. Turn my heart toward you in worship. May my thoughts and actions be pleasing to you. You are worthy of my whole life.

WONDERFUL GIFTS

"If you, imperfect as you are, know how to lovingly take care of your children and give them what's best, how much more ready is your heavenly Father to give wonderful gifts to those who ask him?"

MATTHEW 7:11 TPT

Good parents, though imperfect, know how to take care of their children. They don't just provide the necessities, but they also build a foundation of love, connection, and discipline. They give insight and correction. They delight in giving their children gifts that bring them joy. A good parent knows what their children need and does what it takes to provide them with it.

God's care for you is even better than what the best parent could provide. He is attentive and kind; he doesn't miss a thing. He doesn't lose his patience with you, and he doesn't misunderstand your motives or actions. He delights in listening to the most mundane details of your day! He doesn't grow bored of your interests or weary of your problems. He loves you completely, and he offers you greater gifts than you can imagine asking for!

Father, thank you for your wonderful care. Show me even more clearly how intricate your love is. Thank you for being so attentive and kind.

Easily Found

The Lord loves seeing justice on the earth.
Anywhere and everywhere you can
find his faithful, unfailing love!

PSALM 33:5 TPT

God's love is not reserved for some and withheld from others. It is freely available to all who seek it. It isn't locked up in a storehouse in a remote place. We don't have to hunt for it, and we don't have to meet a list of requirements to be eligible for it. God's love is found anywhere and everywhere! No matter where we are, we can find his faithful and unfailing love.

God delights in showering his love on his children. He doesn't want you to strive or perform for his attention. There is no need! He loves you already, and he sees you exactly as you are. He knows your needs, and he lovingly cares for you. Will you open your heart to your heavenly Father today? Knowing him is the greatest gift you will ever receive.

Lord, I'm so glad that you are always with me. I open my heart to you and ask you to give me a fresh revelation of your love. Align my thoughts with yours and fill my heart with truth.

Spirit Led

Teach me to do your will,
for you are my God;
may your good Spirit
lead me on level ground.

PSALM 143:10 NIV

We have not been brought into the kingdom of God and then abandoned to our own devices. We aren't expected to figure it all out on our own. We have been given the Holy Spirit who is our ever-present helper. He reminds us of the truth, and he gently leads us toward the presence of God. The Spirit is our counselor, our comforter, our teacher, and our guide.

Have you been striving to do God's will yet feel you are coming up short? You can give up the fight for perfection. You don't have to get it right every time. It's important to know that you won't. This does not mean you are failing! God is fully aware of your weaknesses and limitations. They do not intimidate him, and he isn't worried about you letting him down. Instead of being so focused on failure or success, learn to trust the daily leading of the Holy Spirit.

Holy Spirit, help me follow you. Teach me how to hear your voice and listen to your instructions. I want my actions to honor the Lord. Keep me steadily on the right path.

Even Better

Our earthly fathers disciplined us for a few years, doing the best they knew how. But God's discipline is always good for us, so that we might share in his holiness.

HEBREWS 12:10 NLT

It isn't hard to find our parents' flaws. We get a front-row seat to their imperfections, and we intimately know their failures. Even the best parents make mistakes. Our initial ideas about discipline come from their example, right or wrong. As we walk with the Lord, we learn that his discipline is perfect. He is kind, faithful, and gentle. It's important to separate our experiences from the truth of who God is.

God's discipline reveals his kindness. He knows exactly what you need, and his execution is perfect. Everything he does in your life is perfect, and none of it stems from an emotional reaction. He corrects you because he knows what is best for you. This does not mean it is comfortable or easy to be corrected, but you can trust that every correction is purposeful and will bear fruit.

Good Father, thank you for your correction. If my perception of you has been clouded by my childhood experiences, please reveal the truth. Help me see you without bias.

Firm Foundation

Love suffers long and is kind; love does not envy;
love does not parade itself, is not puffed up.

1 Corinthians 13:4 NKJV

Love is the strongest force in the universe. If we think love is a fluffy, ephemeral feeling, we have much to learn about this essential characteristic of God. The very nature of God is love! God's love is long-suffering and kind. It is not envious, and it is not puffed up. Everything he does stems from his great love. It is the firm foundation that all of creation sits upon.

Love is not fleeting or fragile. It can face opposition and remain completely unchanged. It cannot be ruined by our negative choices, and it won't shatter if it's handled incorrectly. It is not delicate or self-centered. God's love for you is steady and perfect. It has the power to impact every area of your life, and it is stronger than you can comprehend. Today, let God's love fill your heart and overflow to those around you.

God, I want to walk in the fullness of your love. I don't want to underestimate its power in my life. Help me love others in the same extravagant way you love me.

Grace upon Grace

From his abundance we have all received one gracious blessing after another.

JOHN 1:16 NLT

No one has reached the limit of God's help. Many of us have barely scratched the surface of his love for us! There will never be a point in our lives when he expects us to be independent from him. We are meant to have continuous fellowship with our Maker. He meets us with compassion every time we turn to him. His grace does not end, and his mercy is consistent. We cannot comprehend all that God has done and all he has in store for us.

If you understood there wasn't a threshold to God's generosity for you, would that change how you approach him? Remember he is delighted by your interaction with him. He loves it when you ask for help. God does not feel disdain or resentment. He doesn't wish you would leave him alone, and his resources aren't taxed by your requests. He has more than enough for everyone. There's no need to be shy or calculated with your prayers. Go boldly before him and trust that he wants to bless you.

Gracious Father, thank you for sharing your abundance with me! Help me understand your generosity on a deeper level. When I have needs, prompt me to come to you first.

BROKENHEARTED

The LORD is near to those who have a broken heart,
And saves such as have a contrite spirit.

PSALM 34:18 NKJV

When we are in pain, we don't have to change a thing to be close to God. He is already near us! Scripture says that he is close to the brokenhearted, and he rushes in to restore the repentant heart. He sees the pain that each of us experiences. He does not ignore it or simply pull us out of it. Instead, he meets us in our brokenness. He comforts us when we cannot take another step forward. He is far more compassionate than we can understand.

You may try to run from your pain, but God does not. It does not make you holier to ignore your heartbreaks and hurts. Be courageous and invite God into that painful place with you. Though the grief is great, it will not consume you because God will not forsake you. He will bring you the comfort of his presence. He will protect you when you are most vulnerable, and he will hold you steady until you can stand again.

God, I'm so glad I don't have to pretend with you. I can come before you just as I am, and you meet me. I need your comfort and your peace. Take my pain and hold me close.

Keep Seeking

"Ask, and the gift is yours. Seek, and you'll discover.
Knock, and the door will be opened for you."

MATTHEW 7:7 TPT

We often complicate that which God has made simple.
Sometimes, the older we get the more we overthink
spiritual matters. We begin to rely on our wisdom, and we
get comfortable with making decisions alone. Our human
definition of maturity and independence doesn't always
line up with how God views those things. We are meant
to embrace our dependence on him; we are meant to
continually ask for help.

Whether your lack of asking comes from pride or
insecurity, let God change your heart. As he reveals your
desperate need for him, respond with humility and gratitude.
He is not a tyrant who demands you do things a certain way.
He is like a loving father who wants the best for his child.
When you seek him, you will be richly blessed.

*Faithful God, I'm done making excuses. I don't want anything
to keep me from searching for you. Strengthen my faith and
teach me how to depend on you.*

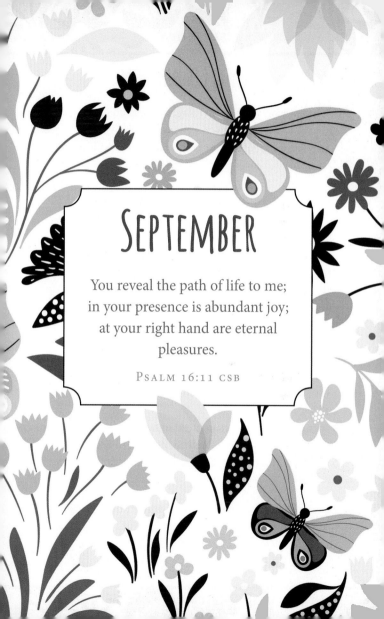

September

You reveal the path of life to me;
in your presence is abundant joy;
at your right hand are eternal
pleasures.

PSALM 16:11 CSB

Daily Connection

Do not worry about anything, but pray and ask God for everything you need, always giving thanks. And God's peace, which is so great we cannot understand it, will keep your hearts and minds in Christ Jesus.

PHILIPPIANS 4:6-7 NCV

Prayer is our connection to God. It is an open line of communication. Our words don't have to be perfect; we don't have to use words at all. God hears the desperate prayers of our hearts as clearly as if we shouted. We can whisper, sing, cry, or yell—it is all the same to him. He isn't offended by our attitudes or frustrated by our emotions. We can offer him our heartfelt requests in any form.

Prayer isn't meant to be a spiritual practice on a holy to-do list. It's meant to be a way for you to stay in fellowship with God. You have the privilege of being in communion with your Maker. Don't overcomplicate it. Simply go to him and welcome him into your day. Talk with him as you would a trusted friend. There's no need to hold back or filter your true feelings. You have complete freedom to bear your soul to him. He is the safest and most capable confidante you will ever have.

Lord, help me keep an open line of prayer flowing from my heart to yours. Reassure me of your love and give me the confidence to ask for what I need.

Pure Hearts

"Blessed are the pure in heart,
for they will see God."

MATTHEW 5:8 CSB

We might read today's verse and wonder how it's possible to have a pure heart. In the Psalms, David asked God to give him a clean heart. He cried out and prayed for a steadfast spirit. We can follow his example, remembering that we are not the ones who do the work. Only God can make our hearts pure. When we feel the error of our ways, or we lack love toward those around us, there is a need for God to renew our hearts.

Your heart is cleansed through the blood of Jesus. He is your salvation, and his sacrifice is what purifies your heart! If you are surrendered in faith to Christ, be assured that your heart is pure. God's work in you makes all the difference! Receive what the Spirit offers and follow his leadership. There is no need to strive for personal perfection; the responsibility is not yours. Lean on Jesus and remember that the work is already done.

God, remove my doubts and remind me that you are the one who makes me clean. Thank you for Christ's sacrifice and the work he did on the cross. When I am discouraged, help me remember that his blood covers me.

Blessed with Trust

The Lord God is a sun and shield;
the Lord bestows favor and honor;
no good thing does he withhold
from those whose walk is blameless.

PSALM 84:11 NIV

The Lord is our sun and shield. He doesn't hold back good gifts from those who seek him. We are instructed to ask for what we need with the full expectation we will receive it. We are meant to ask, seek, and knock at the door of his kingdom. All who do are blessed! The more our trust grows, the more confident we will be in the love of God. He always comes through, and he does not fail.

Don't overthink things today. If you are in Christ, you can confidently walk in his love and favor. This doesn't mean your life will be all sunshine and roses; that's not what Jesus promised. The eternal security and the peace that comes from following Jesus are far better than any circumstantial goodness you could experience in this life. There is fullness found in your relationship with him. As you yield to his leadership and walk in his love you will be blessed with a life that bears abundant fruit.

Lord Almighty, I trust you to move in mercy and lead me in truth. Thank you for the fruit you've produced in my life.

He Comes Through

Then the women said to Naomi, "Blessed be the Lord, who has not left you this day without a redeemer, and may his name be renowned in Israel!"

RUTH 4:14 ESV

Naomi had been widowed and had also recently lost both her sons. She had no one left but her daughters-in-law. One of them, Ruth, couldn't bear to part from Naomi. She accompanied her on the journey back to Naomi's homeland, Moab. Upon reaching Moab, Naomi, which means sweet, asked those who knew her to call her Mara, which means bitter. She felt the bitterness of her grief and abandonment. Today's Scripture outlines the joy that was felt when Boaz redeemed Ruth and Noami.

Scripture is full of accounts that are meant to teach you about the character of God. Read Ruth and be encouraged. God is faithful and he takes care of his children. He will not leave you or forsake you in your time of need. He sees your situation, and he wants to help. The path he has you on may not look like you expected, but you can trust he sees the big picture. Lean on him for support and guidance even when your vision is clouded by bitterness and grief.

Lord, you are the great Redeemer. You restore every broken heart including mine. Encourage me today and keep my eyes on you in every season of the soul.

Faithful and True

He who calls you is faithful; he will do it.

1 Thessalonians 5:24 csb

Promises lose value when they are not backed up by action. When someone's actions line up with their words, we trust them. Trust is a vital part of any relationship. If we cannot count on others to do what they say, there is no chance for honest trust to develop. When we show that we care about someone by being honest and clear, honoring our commitments, and admitting when we're wrong, we build strong and reliable connections.

God is competent, and he follows through on all his promises. He doesn't ever miss the mark. Your patience may be tested as you wait for him to move, but his faithfulness does not depend on your belief. He is true to his word despite your weaknesses or flaws. You can fully trust him because he has proven his ability to do what he says. Today, think of a time in your life when God has met your needs. When you doubt his goodness, remember what he has already done and be encouraged.

Faithful One, you are trustworthy and true. When I grow tired of waiting, remind me of your faithfulness. I rely on your promises. Fill me with new hope as I lean on you.

Showered in Goodness

How great is the goodness
you have stored up for those who fear you.
You lavish it on those who come to you for protection,
blessing them before the watching world.

PSALM 31:19 NLT

We are lavished in goodness when we fear God. He blesses us generously and extravagantly. The treasures that he has in store for those who trust in him are beyond our understanding. The greatest riches the world has to offer pale in comparison to the blessings we will receive from God. Following him is worth every ounce of surrender we have. There is nothing we can muster up for ourselves that is worth missing what God offers us.

Have you ever grown weary in your walk with the Lord? Maybe you're growing tired of saying no to the world or wondering if it's all worth it. Be encouraged, beloved. You aren't running a race in vain. There is a great and glorious prize. Let God strengthen you today. Lift up your weary eyes and fall into his presence. Remember that he is your portion, and he is worthy of your praise.

Lord, thank you for the treasures you store up for those who honor you. I surrender my heart to you. Revive my spirit today and give me perseverance. I trust that I will see your goodness in my life.

Forever Free

"Truly, truly, I say to you, the one who hears My word, and believes Him who sent Me, has eternal life, and does not come into judgment, but has passed out of death into life."

JOHN 5:24 NASB

There is no condemnation for those who are in Christ. He has removed our guilt and our shame. He has liberated us with his love! If we believe in him, we don't have to walk on eggshells. There is no need to wonder if he is mad at us or disappointed by our weaknesses. We have complete and total access to his grace. He sees us with mercy at all times.

If you have committed your life to Christ, you have received the gift of eternal life. You are empowered by his Spirit to walk in freedom. No matter what goes on in the world around you, or in your own life, God is faithful. Your place in his kingdom is sure, and there is mercy for you to start each day with new strength. Don't stay needlessly bound to sin and death. In Christ, you have been set free from anything that would separate you from God.

Jesus Christ, you have removed my guilt, fear, and shame. You have given me a new life, and I am thankful. Help me walk in freedom. I trust that your work on the cross was final and complete.

HEART OF WORSHIP

"From now on, worshiping the Father will not be a matter of
the right place but with a right heart. For God is a Spirit, and
he longs to have sincere worshipers who adore him in the
realm of the Spirit and in truth."

JOHN 4:23-24 TPT

One of the most liberating things about God's love
is that it meets us wherever we are, both physically and
emotionally. We don't have to climb holy mountains or go to
sacred temples to worship the Lord. We worship in spirit and
truth when we offer him our surrendered hearts in any place
and on any day. Our adoration toward God has taken the
place of meeting the impossible standard of the law.

If you consider yourself a perfectionist, the idea of not
having to prove your worth might be a stumbling block for
you. Conversely, you might find great relief knowing that
you are off the hook. Either way, remember that true worship
has nothing to do with the circumstances surrounding it.
You can offer your heart to the Lord, no matter how messy
it is, and know that it delights him. Nothing stands between
you and consistent fellowship with God.

*God, thank you for making a way to worship you at all times.
I'm so glad I don't have to follow a list of rules. I give my heart
to you today. Take it and make me more like you.*

Give Freely

"Give, and it will be given to you: good measure, pressed down, shaken together, and running over will be put into your bosom. For with the same measure that you use, it will be measured back to you."

LUKE 6:38 NKJV

God is generous, and his resources are abundant. He is not lacking in anything. Whatever we ask for, we can be sure that God is capable of doing it. He loves to bless those who mirror his generosity. When we give to others, we make room to receive more from God. One of the most beautiful principles of his kingdom is the more we give, the more we receive.

Generosity can be practiced in every aspect of your life from finances to friendship. Many in this world hold tightly to what they have, only using it to serve themselves. Instead of following the ways of the world, give freely. Remember that God has better gifts in store for you than what you can hoard for yourself. Generosity is often an act of faith. As a believer, you hold your blessings loosely because you know it is only by God's grace that you have them in the first place.

Generous Father, I don't want to be stingy. I want to generously share what you so freely give to me. Thank you for your guidance as I am growing in this area.

Growth and Change

We do not enjoy being disciplined. It is painful at the time,
but later, after we have learned from it, we have peace,
because we start living in the right way.

HEBREWS 12:11 NCV

No one likes to be corrected. As believers, we must
change our perspective if we want to grow in maturity.
When we see correction as a tool for growing in wisdom, we
can welcome it without being defensive. God's correction
is merciful and kind. He not only lovingly points out what
needs to be repaired, he fully equips us to do it. He is gentle,
strong, and the perfect teacher.

One day, Jesus will return and make all things new.
In his presence, you will be transformed into his likeness.
Anything that is broken will be made whole. Until that day,
you will have to embrace humility and continue learning.
Trust God to lead you on the right path. He knows exactly
what you need to learn and how you need to learn it. Lean
on his leadership and stay open to growth and change.

*Perfect One, I humbly offer my life to you. May your will be
done. Show me areas in need of growth and equip me to do it.
I don't want to resist your correction. I trust your leadership.*

Pleasant Portion

My flesh and my heart may fail,
but God is the strength of my heart,
my portion forever.

PSALM 73:26 CSB

What an incredible gift it is to know the powerful
presence of God in every season and situation. He is our
pleasant portion, yesterday, today, and forever. He will
not fail us! If we need anything, we can find it in him. He
will fortify our hearts, and he will strengthen us with his
generous grace. He will comfort us with his strong embrace.

When your body fails, you can still experience
incredible strength in the Lord. He remains your plentiful
portion of peace, no matter what you are going through.
Your worth is not in what you can do, but in who you belong
to. Your identity is wrapped up in the mercy and kindness
of your heavenly Father. He will never turn away from you
when you look toward him.

*Father, wrap me in your arms of your mercy. Strengthen my
heart in your presence. You are my portion now and forever.*

Radiant Light

This is the message we have heard from him and declare
to you: God is light; in him there is no darkness at all.

1 John 1:5 niv

God sees all, knows all, and is completely perfect. There
is no failure or fault in him. There is no shadow of doubt in
him. He is full of faithfulness, and he is radiant with love.
God is pure light, and he brings life to all under his gaze.
Like the earth and all of its inhabitants are dependent on the
light of the sun, so are all people dependent on the light of
God to sustain us!

You don't need to fear what lurks in the shadows of
your life. When God's light shines on you, he lights up
even the darkest corners of your heart. What once felt
mysterious, overwhelming, or even tinged with fear becomes
manageable as you bask in the compassion of God's gaze.
Just as the light of day allows you to see the world more
clearly, so does the light of God's love open your eyes to
truth and beauty!

*Radiant One, I bask in the light of your presence today. Shine on
every area of my life and show me how I can be more like you.*

In God's Hands

Do not repay evil for evil or reviling for reviling, but on the contrary, bless, for to this you were called, that you may obtain a blessing.

1 PETER 3:9 ESV

The ways of God's kingdom truly are different from our self-protective nature. It is natural for us to want to lash out at those who hurt us, but that is not God's way. Instead, he asks us to leave justice and vindication in his hands. He is the perfect judge who is capable of having mercy in every situation. We are free to let him fight our battles while we practice loving others as Christ loves us.

Jesus' love met you when you were lost in your sin. He didn't make you pay for your wrongs, and he didn't throw your mistakes in your face. He loved you in a self-sacrificing way, taking your burdens upon himself. You can practice self-sacrificial love in small ways. When someone says something unkind, return a blessing instead of a mean remark. When you are wronged, surrender the situation to God. Let him handle it. A day is coming when God will make all the wrong things right. Until then, don't store up resentment in your heart. Leave justice in the hands of God and rest in the freedom you've been given.

Lord, fill me with your love today so I love others well. Help me have mercy on others as you've had mercy on me.

Power and Strength

He gives power to the weak
and strength to the powerless.

ISAIAH 40:29 NLT

God's kindness extends to every part of our lives. His love for us is great, and his generosity reflects how much he cares. We don't have to earn his favor or pray the right prayer to receive his help. He knows us fully, and he sees the intentions of our hearts. Even when we feel weak and powerless, God reaches out to us with the power and strength of his love!

Whatever you need today, God is capable of providing it. Turn toward him and he will not ignore you. If he says he will give power to the weak you can be sure he will do it. There isn't a list of prerequisites you must meet. When you ask, he will provide for you in whatever way is best. He may meet a tangible and practical need, or he might bless you with the endurance needed to get through a trial. He may encourage you with a divine word, or he may orchestrate an experience that lifts your spirit. No matter what it looks like, God will provide for you.

Mighty God, I'm so grateful you meet me when I am week. Thank you for giving me strength when I cannot go on. Help me rely on you at all times.

No Fear

There is no fear in love, but perfect love drives out fear,
because fear involves punishment, and the one who fears is
not perfected in love.

1 John 4:18 nasb

When it comes to fear, we often think of stereotypes.
We're afraid of spiders, heights, storms, or small spaces.
We think of physical threats like driving on busy highways
or being overwhelmed by a crowd. While God absolutely
delivers us from tangible fears, he also brings freedom from
the fears that are more difficult to pinpoint. He liberates us
from the fears that hide deep in our hearts.

If you allow him to, God can bring healing to the
parts of your heart that have been ruled by fear. If you
find yourself worried about hypothetical situations, lay
your burdens before the King. He sees you with so much
compassion and kindness. Whether you're afraid of being
alone, not measuring up, or how other people see you, God's
love can bring freedom. God can handle every insecurity,
anxiety, and stress.

*God, thank you for your generous love, which frees me from
fear's grip. I surrender my deepest insecurities to you. Fill my
heart with your love and help me experience freedom.*

Sing Praises

Sing praises to the Lord, for he has done marvelous wonders,
and let his fame be known throughout the earth!
Give out a shout of cheer; sing for joy, O people of Zion,
for great and mighty is the Holy One of Israel who lives
among you!

ISAIAH 12:5 TPT

Worship is both a salve and a weapon. It brings us peace and strength. Through worship, we can find healing and make space for God to reveal truth to our spirits. When we sing praises to him, we align our hearts with his, and we posture ourselves to receive from him. Declaring the truth aloud is powerful and impactful.

Sing praises to the Lord today. Lay your burdens at his altar and seek to minister to his heart. Tell him what you love about him. Thank him for specific things he's done for you. Rejoice over his goodness and find delight in his presence. As you look toward him in praise, he will soften your heart and speak to your spirit. Time spent in worship is never wasted.

God, I sing for joy because of your faithfulness. I delight in you, for you have been good to me! Receive my praises today as I pour out my love offering to you!

SEATED WITH HIM

He raised us from the dead along with Christ and seated us with him in the heavenly realms because we are united with Christ Jesus.

EPHESIANS 2:6 NLT

We have received the infinite riches of God's grace and kindness through Christ. We are seated with Jesus in the heavenly realms. We cannot do anything to earn this position and none of us deserves it in any way. Without Jesus, we would have no way of getting to God. We are completely at the mercy of our Savior. Praise God his mercy abounds!

God has good things planned for those who follow him. One day, you will experience the fullness of his presence. It will be a glorious day! While you wait for the coming perfection, remember that Christ's sacrifice gives you hope. When it seems like things will never get better, remember that the same power that raised him from the dead lives in you.

Gracious God, you are worthy of all my praise! Thank you for the new life I have in Jesus and for the position you've given me in your kingdom. Help me persevere until I am with you forever.

Close To All

The LORD is close to everyone who prays to him,
to all who truly pray to him.

PSALM 145:18 NCV

Prayer keeps us connected to God. Scripture assures us that God hears our cries and is faithful to answer us. He is near to all who call on him. When we pray, we posture our hearts in humility before the Lord. We admit we need help and acknowledge that God's ways are higher than our own. Prayer is an act of worship in itself.

Anyone can build a strong practice of prayer. If you are struggling to know where to start, look at Scripture. It is full of examples of how to pray. Throughout the Word, you'll see accounts of people pouring their hearts out to the Lord. Some are poetic and well-organized, while others are raw and full of intense emotion. Either option is great as long as you are authentically offering your heart to God. He loves it when you come to him just as you are. Reach out to him and he will be near to you.

God, I want to be in constant communion with you. I come to you with all my burdens and praises. Be near to me as I pour my heart out to you.

Wisdom and Knowledge

In him are hidden all the treasures
of wisdom and knowledge.

COLOSSIANS 2:3 CSB

The wisdom of God is always applicable to our lives.
It is as practical as it is spiritual. God loves to break down
the mysteries of his heart in attainable ways. He not only
provides salvation for our souls, but he also gives us an
abundance of wise instruction on how to live. Everything
God says is right and useful. If he tells us to live a certain
way, we can be sure it is best for us. He doesn't give arbitrary
directions or throw meaningless rules at us.

God has not left you to flail in the face of problems.
Everything you need for living is found in his presence and
through his Word. Remain surrendered to him and he will
faithfully direct you on the right path. No matter what your
circumstances are, you can seek God for what you need.
Wherever you find yourself today, his wisdom is available
and relevant.

*Wise God, I don't want to foolishly think I know better than
you do. I submit to your wisdom and your ways. Lead me on
and reveal the treasures of your heart.*

INCREDIBLE KINDNESS

God can point to us in all future ages as examples
of the incredible wealth of his grace and kindness
toward us, as shown in all he has done for us who
are united with Christ Jesus.

EPHESIANS 2:7 NLT

When we surrendered at the cross, we united ourselves
with Jesus. As such, our lives are examples of the wealth of
God's grace and kindness. It is his abundant goodness that
restored our souls. He is the one who made a way for us to
be with him forever. Out of his great love, we are redeemed.
When people observe our lives, they should see a reflection
of God's love for all humanity.

God has been so exceedingly kind to you. He has lifted
you out of sin and shame and given you a place at his table.
He has provided you with everything you need in this life
and the next. In him, you lack nothing. You have a place
in his kingdom that cannot be stolen from you. You have
been adopted into his family and will always belong in his
presence. Your heavenly Father has ensured your safety and
provision forever.

Heavenly Father, I am so thankful for all you've done for me.
May my life reflect your love. Give me a greater understanding
of your grace and help me display it well.

Call To Worship

Happy are those who hear the joyful call to worship,
for they will walk in the light of your presence, Lord.

PSALM 89:15 NLT

As believers, we can hear the joyful call to worship
in every season of our lives. It is not reserved for times
of feasting or celebration. God invites us to worship in
every circumstance and during every struggle! Worship
is a powerful tool that can give us a fresh perspective and
respite from our troubles. Worship born out of brokenness is
powerful and poignant.

You can choose to see every opportunity as a platform
for praise. When you hear disappointing news, turn it over
to the Lord. When an unexpected interruption leads you in
a different direction than anticipated, thank God for the joy
of flexibility. There are endless opportunities to praise God if
you look for them. Happy are those who hear this call. Today,
open your heart and enjoy offering your praise to God.

*Lord, turn my disappointments into joy. You are worthy of
all my praise. I offer you my heart and look forward to the
redemption you will bring. Keep my eyes on you and help me
answer your joyful call to worship.*

Tired and Weary

Even youths shall faint and be weary,
and young men shall fall exhausted.

ISAIAH 40:30 ESV

No one can opt out of their humanity. We all grow weary and tired. Even the strongest and most youthful among us need to rest. Instead of punishing ourselves, let's embrace our God-given need for rest and nourishment. Weariness does not equate to failure. The ability to slow down when needed shows maturity and discipline. Sometimes it's harder to stop working than to start.

Embrace your frailty and invite God into your weaknesses. As you wait upon the Lord, he will renew your strength. When weariness overcomes you there is no need to push through. Exhaustion is an indicator to rest, refresh, and recover. God's love for you is not based on your ability to perform. Resting in his mercy and waiting upon him is good for your body and soul. He will renew you and give you the strength you need.

God, thank you for the invitation to rest when I am weary. I don't want to find my worth in my ability to work. Instead, help me lay down my burdens and trust that your strength is greater than mine.

Good Medicine

A cheerful heart is good medicine,
but a broken spirit saps a person's strength.

PROVERBS 17:22 NLT

How many of us are walking around with broken spirits? Our culture has normalized the consistent presence of stress and overwhelm. It's so pervasive that sometimes we don't recognize that there are other options. God did not intend for his children to be weary, defeated, and full of despair. He longs for us to experience the goodness that is found in his presence. Whether we are in the habit of embracing pessimism, or our tired souls need deep refreshing, God can lift us up.

Let your kind Father minister to your heart today. Don't be ashamed of your brokenness but allow him to bring restoration to your soul. If you are tired and weary, he can give you rest. If you are lost in despair, he can shine his light on the darkest parts of your mind. If you can't remember when you last felt happy, let his joy be like medicine to your soul. Lift your eyes toward him today and let him revive you in a new way.

Lord, thank you for the comfort of your presence and for the wonderful gift of joy that soothes my wounded heart. Please meet me as I am and minister to my heart today.

New Things

If anyone is in Christ, this person is a new creation; the old
things passed away; behold, new things have come.

2 Corinthians 5:17 nasb

Who doesn't love the thrill of a new start? Change
can be hard, but a fresh beginning is also exciting and full
of promise. The Word says the mercies of the Lord are
new every morning. Each day is an opportunity for us to
experience God's love in a fresh way. We don't have to carry
yesterday's mistakes on our shoulders. We can rely on him
for mercy and move forward unhindered by the past.

Each sunrise brings renewal and fresh hope. When
you open your eyes in the morning, remember that God is
offering you a fresh start. He has given you breath in your
lungs, and a new day lies ahead. Don't be discouraged by
yesterday's problems or plagued by tomorrow's potential
worries. Lean on the mercy of God and trust that he makes
everything new in his perfect timing.

*Jesus, thank you for making me new. Thank you for the mercy
you so freely give. Fill me with hope as you make me more
like you.*

God Can

Looking into their eyes, Jesus replied, "Humanly speaking, no one, because no one can save himself. But what seems impossible to you is never impossible to God!"

MATTHEW 19:26 TPT

No matter how good we are, we cannot save ourselves. Even if we have the best intentions, we still fall short of God's perfection. We need his grace and unending mercy. God's grace is given freely, and it is offered to everyone in the same portion. When we approach him, we all receive the same blessings.

It is God's delight to save you. He doesn't begrudgingly offer grace. He isn't annoyed by your weaknesses, and he doesn't look down on your inability to save yourself. He loves offering you his strength, peace, and love. Instead of striving for what you can never achieve, lean on the Lord and rest. Take a deep breath and let thanksgiving fill your heart. God has done great things for you.

God, I am helpless without your grace. Help me look past my imperfections and trust you fully for salvation. You are the only one who offers true hope. Thank you for all you've done.

Spring Forth

As the earth brings forth its bud,
As the garden causes the things
that are sown in it to spring forth,
So the LORD God will cause righteousness
and praise to spring forth before all the nations.

ISAIAH 61:11 NKJV

The weather goes through seasonal shifts, and so do we. Our lives shift and change as time goes by. We do not live in perpetual winter. Cold, dark, and hopeless nights won't last forever. Conversely, we don't get to experience endless summer days. Flowers won't bloom eternally, and the sky won't always be blue. Change is inevitable. No matter what we go through, good, or bad, it cannot last forever.

God knows exactly what you need and when you need it. When trials arise, don't despair. God will faithfully lead you through it. There may even be blessings on the other side. Remember that he knows each season you will walk through. Just as he controls the coming and going of spring or winter, so he controls the shifting seasons of your life. He is sovereign, and he is trustworthy.

God, I trust your timing. You are in control, and I am happy to put my life in your hands. As I walk through this season of life, help me lean on you and trust your plans. You are faithful and worthy of my praise.

Remember Him

Remember the LORD in all you do,
and he will give you success.

PROVERBS 3:6 NCV

As Christians, we are called to remember the Lord in all we do. This means that our walk with God requires intentionality. It doesn't happen by accident, and we won't stumble into it. God has given us free will and we must choose what or who we will worship. If we don't deliberately put God on the pedestal of our lives, we will inevitably worship something else. Money, work, relationships, material possessions, and personal satisfaction can all take the place of God in our lives.

You were made to worship your Maker. You will only be truly satisfied when you are satisfied in his presence. He offers you all you need. He created you, and he knows you inside and out. The world cannot offer you success like God can. God's success is fulfilling and eternal. As you include him in the details of your life you will find that his favor follows you wherever you go. A life that is surrendered to the King will bear much fruit.

Lord, I want to honor you in all I do. I invite you to be involved in my day. I want you to be part of every detail of my life. Guide me and keep me close to your heart.

Cheerful Giver

Each person should do as he has decided in his heart—
not reluctantly or out of compulsion,
since God loves a cheerful giver.

2 CORINTHIANS 9:7 CSB

God is a cheerful giver. He delights in generously offering us his love, peace, joy, and salvation. As dearly beloved children, we reflect the nature of our Father when we choose to live generously in this world. We willingly share the blessings we've been given because we know they came from God. Every good thing in our lives comes from his hands. When we hold those gifts loosely and share them joyfully, we honor the Lord.

Today, take a moment to check your heart. Are your generous actions accompanied by joy and cheerfulness? Or are the gifts you give laced with hidden frustration and bitterness? God cares about how you feel. He wants you to experience the lightness that comes from joyfully sharing his gifts with others. Let him transform your heart. If you allow him to, he will faithfully turn bitterness into delight.

Generous One, thank you for the lavish gifts you've given me. I am moved by your generosity and kindness. Help me give as cheerfully as you do. I trust you to take care of me.

Ask and Receive

"Everyone who asks receives; the one who seeks finds;
and to the one who knocks, the door will be opened."

MATTHEW 7:8 NIV

God is earnest in his love for us. He sees us clearly,
opens his hands, and satisfies every living thing. He knows
exactly what we need and how to provide it. He hears our
cries, and he is faithful to answer us. He does not hide, play
games, or belittle us for needing help. He doesn't answer our
honest requests with cruel jokes. He doesn't ignore our needs
or make us suffer for our weaknesses.

Ask God for what you need. It's so simple, it's
revolutionary. Do you need peace, a new job, or wisdom in
dealing with a conflict? Do you need a minute to watch the
sunset, salvation for a loved one, or help with a work project?
There is nothing in your life that is too big or too small to
bring to God. He wants to be part of all of it. He loves it
when you include him in the monumental and the mundane.
Invite him to walk with you today.

*Father, you have been so good to me! I don't want to struggle
through my day when I could ask you for help. Meet me where
I am weak and give me the strength I need. I lay my burdens
at your feet today.*

HIDING PLACE

You are a hiding place for me;
you preserve me from trouble;
you surround me with shouts of deliverance.

PSALM 32:7 ESV

God offers us a hiding place within his presence. When we need a place to safely breathe, we can run to God. When we cannot see through the storm, there is shelter in his arms. When we are weary from a never-ending fight, he offers a place of respite. No catastrophe or disaster can keep us from God's peace and deliverance.

Finding refuge in God's presence takes practice. It's easy to forget that it's even an option. In the hustle and bustle of everyday life, you might not even realize you have a need for rest and quiet. Today, take a moment to bask in the safety of his arms. Make a habit of letting him renew your spirit multiple times a day. When you run to him, he will fill you afresh with peace, love, and the perseverance you need for the day.

Most High, you are my rock of refuge and the secret place where I can hide. Help me remember that you are always available. Prompt my spirit to find rest in you throughout my day.

OCTOBER

Take delight in the LORD,
and he will give you
your heart's desires.

PSALM 37:4 NLT

Love Over Law

The purpose of my instruction is that all believers would
be filled with love that comes from a pure heart, a clear
conscience, and genuine faith.

1 TIMOTHY 1:5 NLT

Paul's letter to Timothy is filled with admonitions to
value love above all else. He urges the church to be more
focused on God's love than on teaching the law. This
problem is not isolated to that period of time. We all know
how easy it is to elevate our opinions over loving others. We
like to be considered wise, and it is tempting to develop the
habit of proving our intelligence with our words.

Rather than making sure everyone around you knows
how smart you are, focus on loving them with kindness,
gentleness, and sincerity. Conversely, if you have been hurt
by someone else's lack of humility, bring your offense to
the Lord. He will hold you gently and comfort your heart.
Whether you've been on the giving or receiving end of
prideful words, God's grace is sufficient.

*God, I want to be known for loving others well. Keep me from
pride and stubbornness. Help me place a higher value on your
love than on being right. Give me discernment to know when
to speak and when to be quiet.*

Numbered Days

Help us to remember that our days are numbered,
and help us to interpret our lives correctly.
Set your wisdom deeply in our hearts
so that we may accept your correction.

PSALM 90:12 TPT

When we remember that our lives on this earth are limited, we can focus on what really matters. It isn't worth it to hoard treasures that will not last. Especially when life seems smooth, it is easy to begin to coast through our days. If we aren't diligent, we are bound to slowly meander toward the path of worldly satisfaction and manufactured comfort. Since none of us knows how much time we have, we should be wise with each of our days.

Have you ever experienced a crisis that made you feel the power of this verse? Suffering and grief often put life into perspective. In the midst of your pain, you might have experienced great clarity. While no one wants to experience trials, it is good to be aware of how fragile and limited life is. As you realize your days are numbered, you have the opportunity to align your values and hopes with God's plans.

God, help me be aware of my time. Give me clarity and teach me how to be wise with the days I am given. Help me honor you every step of the way. I want to focus on what really matters.

TROUBLED HEARTS

"Do not let your heart be troubled;
believe in God, believe also in Me."

JOHN 14:1 NASB

When the disciples realized Jesus would be leaving them, they were distressed. He told them not to let their hearts be troubled. He knew exactly how God's plan would unfold. The disciples were discouraged because they had a limited view of the future. Though he spoke in vague, prophetic terms about what was coming, Jesus's Words were laced with compassion and encouragement. He didn't demean them for not understanding, and he didn't shove their feelings aside. His words were gentle, kind, and hopeful.

When you feel twinges of discomfort about the future, lean on God's faithfulness. Remind yourself how trustworthy he is. Keep believing that God will lead you through every challenge you face. Instead of drowning in worry, turn your thoughts toward him. He will encourage you, and he will provide for you. Today, may you know the comfort of trusting him when your heart is troubled.

Faithful Lord, I believe in your promises. I trust your steadfast nature to lead me through each trial I face. Even when I don't understand the future, I know that you are faithful. I look to you today for peace and hope.

Stronger and Wiser

Though an army may encamp against me,
My heart shall not fear;
Though war may rise against me,
In this I will be confident.

PSALM 27:3 NKJV

Even when we face opposition, we don't need to be afraid. We can rest in God's faithfulness. He will keep us safe through every battle! Even when we are surrounded and cannot see a way out, God does not panic. No matter what our circumstances look like, he is capable of rescuing us. He is stronger and wiser than our fiercest enemies. Whether we struggle with other people, unexpected trials, or our own weaknesses, God can see us through every situation.

Scripture reassures you that even if everyone in your life forsakes you, God will take care of you. His strength is enough for you. He walks with you faithfully, and he is aware of every problem you face. He will never leave you or abandon you. Invite him into your day and pour your heart out to him. Call out to him and expect him to show up. Let your heart find assurance in God's ability to meet you, save you, and lift you up.

Lord, you are my strength and my faithful shield. Rescue me from my trials and help me rely on your strength. Thank you for showing up when I need you most.

Clothed in Love

Even more than all this, clothe yourself in love.
Love is what holds you all together in perfect unity.

COLOSSIANS 3:14 NCV

Love is the highest law of God's kingdom. It is the very essence of who he is. Everything God does stems from his good and perfect love. As his beloved heirs, we are meant to display that love for all to see. We share God's love when we choose to remain gentle and humble in our interactions with others. We embody his love when we are slow to anger and quick to forgive. Whenever our character reflects him, we teach the world who God really is.

Choosing to clothe yourself in God's love means that you will stand out from others. Your actions and demeanor won't always line up with what is popular or socially accepted. Instead of being quick to take offense, or eager to elevate your own opinion, seek to be gracious and merciful. Let your gentle words point others to the gentle heart of Christ. Don't be afraid to stand out when loving others is your motivation.

Lord, your love is strong and life changing. I want to clothe myself in your love every day so I can share it with those around me. Help me faithfully love others as you do.

HEALER

He heals the brokenhearted
and bandages their wounds.

PSALM 147:3 CSB

We cannot escape the effects of heartbreak. We all experience loss and are faced with grief we don't know how to handle. At some point or another, each of us will walk through a great and painful trial. No amount of wealth, preparedness, or intellect can shield any of us from suffering. While we are all brought low by pain, we are also all lifted up by God's love. He attends to the wounds of those whose hearts are shattered. He is faithful to those who are hurting.

Whatever hurts you carry, each is an opportunity to know the healing power of God's presence. Run to him and show him your wounds. No matter how gaping or grotesque they are, he can heal you. He wants to be close to you. He wants to comfort you, and he wants to give you new hope. He knows exactly what you need, and he will expertly care for each of your infirmities.

My Healer, thank you for the opportunity to know you more through my greatest wounds. Flood my heart with your love and light up the dark corners of my mind. I trust that you will take care of me perfectly. Thank you for the comfort of your presence.

Delight in Waiting

"What delight comes to you when you wait upon the Lord!
For you will find what you long for."

Matthew 5:4 tpt

Waiting is an act of faith. We wait for something because we believe we will get it. If there is no endpoint or promise of reward, we don't wait. No one stands in a line that leads nowhere or goes on a pilgrimage without a destination. The very act of waiting means that we are trusting God for something specific. This delights his heart, and he is faithful to reward us with his presence.

When you wait on God you are communicating that you trust he will come through. Your faith is strengthened as you rely on his promises. While you wait, God will meet you. He will be with you every step of the way. No matter how long you are waiting, he won't abandon you. In his presence, you will find peace, perseverance, and strength.

God, thank you for your presence that brings peace, clarity, encouragement, and joy. Please stay with me as I wait for your promises to be fulfilled. You have been faithful in my life, and I trust you will continue to be.

Called to Freedom

You, my brothers and sisters, were called to be free.
But do not use your freedom to indulge the flesh;
rather, serve one another humbly in love.

GALATIANS 5:13 NIV

God offers us true freedom, and we get to decide what
to do with it. He does not force us into obedience or give
us a list of requirements we must meet. At the same time,
Scripture is clear that it is best for us to follow God's ways.
We have been given an abundance of grace and our response
should be to honor God in all we do.

There is a balancing act in the Christian life. Your
response to grace should be devotion, but your devotion
should not be defined by striving for perfection. You cannot
do anything to earn God's favor. If your good deeds stem
from fear or self-preservation, then you might not fully
understand the freedom God offers you. Ask the Holy Spirit
to open your eyes and give you understanding. Soften your
heart and receive what God has for you.

*Savior, I want to walk in the fullness of freedom. Show me if
there are areas in my life where I am indulging my flesh or
striving for perfection. Help me honor you rightly. Give me an
understanding of what it means to receive your grace.*

Humble and Soft

"Love your enemies, and do good, and lend, expecting nothing in return, and your reward will be great, and you will be sons of the Most High, for he is kind to the ungrateful and the evil."

LUKE 6:35 ESV

Christ's sacrifice covers each of our inequities without discrimination or bias. There is nothing we can do to earn his affection, and there is nothing we can do to be deemed unworthy of his love. As such, we should freely offer his love to everyone we meet. It is difficult to be merciful to others when we are unaware of the great mercy we've received. Our humility and recognition of our own shortcomings allow us to be gracious to others when they stumble or fall.

You will have a difficult time loving others if you are convinced of your own perfection. If you think you are more deserving of grace than anyone else, this is a red flag that you need to adjust your mindset. God's faithfulness does not depend on your good behavior. He offers you salvation on your very worst day. It's possible there will be a day in your life when you find yourself in a position you never imagined. We are all prone to sin and capable of falling. Humbly accept God's grace and seek to keep your heart soft toward others.

God, give me a fresh revelation of your grace. I don't want to take it for granted or forget that I am undeserving.

Always Seen

God is not unjust. He will not forget how hard you have
worked for him and how you have shown your love to him
by caring for other believers, as you still do.

HEBREWS 6:10 NLT

It can be discouraging when our efforts are overlooked.
It is not glamorous to serve behind the scenes, and it can be
hurtful when we aren't recognized for the work we've done.
The good news is that the kingdom of God operates under
different rules than the world. In God's kingdom, the unseen
are highly valued. God sees what we do in the background. He
knows the choices we make when no one else is looking, and
he will honor our generosity and service. We can be sure of it!

God is your greatest advocate and encourager. When
you are working for his approval, you will always be satisfied.
He sees everything you do, and he will adequately reward
you. There is no need to despair when others don't take
notice. If you find yourself saddened by a lack of attention,
let it be an opportunity to be lifted up by God rather than
the words of others. He will not forget you, and his opinion
matters most.

*God, your approval is all I want. You don't ignore or overlook
my hard work. I trust that you will reward me for the good
I've done. Thank you for seeing me and encouraging me.*

Confidence before Him

This is the confidence which we have before Him, that,
if we ask anything according to His will, He hears us.

1 John 5:14 NASB

When our prayers align with God's will, he hears us.
This is a definitive truth. His ears are turned toward our
cries, and he is familiar with our voices. He knows who
we are and what we need. Our individual requests don't
get lost in a sea of problems. He doesn't have a waiting list,
and he doesn't prioritize one person over the other. God
miraculously hears each of us, and he is fully capable of
meeting all of our needs.

If you are unsure of what to pray, look at the Word. The
more familiar you are with God's character and wisdom, the
more confident you will become in discerning his will. As
you gain confidence, your prayers will align with his desires.
You are fully equipped to understand God's will. It's not a
mystery that cannot be solved. He has given you all the tools
you need.

*Merciful Father, thank you for hearing my prayers. Help me
understand your will. I want my desires to line up with yours.
Thank you for revealing yourself through your Word.*

Eternal Life

Eternal life means to know and experience you
as the only true God,
and to know and experience Jesus Christ,
as the Son whom you have sent.

JOHN 17:3 TPT

When we spend eternity in God's presence, we will fully experience his goodness. We experience glimpses of that goodness now, but even our best days don't compare to the perfection that is coming. In the space between promise and fulfillment, we can experience the overwhelming power of God's love. While we wait for eternity, we can lean on the comfort and guidance of the Holy Spirit. Every moment of goodness or restoration is a glimpse into how God intended things to be.

Let the promise of eternal life motivate you to stay faithful to God. On your worst days, remember that a day will come when every tear is wiped away. You will live joyfully with your maker, and every sorrow will disappear. You will be fully restored, and you will see the full perfection of God's great plan for humanity. Take heart because your struggles will not last forever.

God, open my eyes to see your goodness. Fill me with anticipation for eternity. Give me perseverance to remain faithful to you as I wait.

Without Hindrance

I love the LORD, because He has heard
My voice and my supplications.
Because He has inclined His ear to me,
Therefore I will call upon Him as long as I live.

PSALM 116:1-2 NKJV

God does not ask us to follow him and then give us nothing in return. He is not demanding or unreasonable. His instructions come with unfathomable rewards. He promises to answer when we call. He will not ignore us when we ask for help. Our weak surrender and devotion are met with his eternal and unshakeable loyalty.

God will never leave you empty-handed. Following him is worth every sacrifice you might make. There is nothing you can give to God that compares with what he has given you. This is cause for great rejoicing! He will never make you feel unworthy, and he will never demean you for your weakness. Even though you have nothing of value to offer, he lifts you up and is eager to give you an eternal inheritance. He welcomes you into his kingdom without hindrance or delay. God's offer of grace is wildly unbalanced, yet he offers it with joy.

God, I delight in your law of love because you have delighted in me. Everything you do is good, kind, and true. Thank you for listening to me and coming to my rescue.

ANY CIRCUMSTANCE

"Do not be afraid, for I have ransomed you.
I have called you by name; you are mine.
When you go through deep waters, I will be with you."

ISAIAH 43:1-2 NLT

God is always with us. He never leaves or forsakes his people. Even if we get ourselves into a mess, he still rescues us. His faithfulness is dependent on his character, not our actions. When we invite him to, he stays by our side and walks with us every step of the way. There is no situation that he cannot lead us through. He blesses us with the comfort of his presence, and he gives us wisdom to know which way to go.

God has given you an incredible invitation. He has made himself available to you in any situation. No matter how dire or difficult it seems, God is able and willing to meet you where you are. There is no other relationship in your life that offers that kind of fierce loyalty. Even your closest friends or your spouse cannot promise their presence to you one hundred percent of the time. Rejoice and take God up on his offer. Allow the King of Kings to escort you through whatever you are facing.

Mighty King, thank you for the power of your presence! I am so thankful that you are with me no matter where I am. Help me rely on your strength and trust your guidance. You can get me through any situation, no matter how impossible it seems.

Simple Prayers

"When you pray, don't babble like the Gentiles, since they imagine they'll be heard for their many words. Don't be like them, because your Father knows the things you need before you ask him."

MATTHEW 6:7-8 CSB

There's nothing wrong with a long prayer, but it's important to understand that longevity is not what holds God's attention. He already knows our needs. We don't have to beg him to answer, and we don't have to make sure every minute detail is perfectly communicated. We are no less holy when our prayers are simple than when they are poetic or refined.

Your communication with God can be as basic as breathing. Remember the value of uttering simple prayers. Don't be distracted by trying to find the perfect words. Trust that God already knows exactly what is in your heart. He doesn't need you to explain it to him. Rather, he is delighted by your desire to commune with him. Let your prayers be natural, free-flowing, and unhindered.

Lord Jesus, thank you for the invitation to pray simply. I don't want to put on a show for you; I only want to know you. Thank you for meeting me throughout my day.

Open Invitation

The Spirit and the bride say, "Come!" And let the one who hears say, "Come!" Let the one who is thirsty come; and let the one who wishes take the free gift of the water of life.

REVELATION 22:17 NIV

This portion of Revelation is an invitation to all who are spiritually thirsty and crave the gift of living water. The way we respond is up to us. Do we want to answer the call? Have we come into the presence of the living God to drink from the well of his lovingkindness? Have we tasted the power of his salvation? The invitation is available to each of us.

God is not demanding. He does not shout for you to obey him. He will not shame you into having a relationship. His invitation is open, and it does not come with a time limit. He calls you with loving-kindness. The more you get to know him, the more you will experience his gentleness and grace. Scripture says that he is the God who opens his hand and satisfies the desires of every living thing. Come and drink from his refreshing fountain today!

God, I answer your call today. Thank you for your gracious invitation to be satisfied in your presence. Refresh me from the inside out. Fill me with your Spirit and revive my soul.

Humble Hearts

Listen, my beloved brothers, has not God chosen those who
are poor in the world to be rich in faith and heirs of the
kingdom, which he has promised to those who love him?

JAMES 2:5 ESV

God does not show favoritism to people. He is not
impressed by prestige or swayed by wealth. It is good to
follow his example and share his love without bias. We are
called to be generous toward those who have nothing to offer
us. Our kindness should not depend on the social status of
others. Though wealth can garner favor in the world, it does
not have the same merit in God's kingdom.

Do you find yourself swayed by the status and social
appeal the world offers? It's easy to become wrapped up
in a desire for earthly satisfaction. Remember that God's
promises are far better than anything the world can offer.
Don't be enticed by riches and material possessions. Instead,
learn to find value in the lowly and forgotten. Follow Christ's
example and elevate those the world has deemed unworthy.

*God, your ways are so much better than the ways of this
world! Help me remain humble and loving to all. I don't want
to be swayed by prestige or presentation.*

Live Freely

Sin is no longer your master, for you no longer live under the requirements of the law. Instead, you live under the freedom of God's grace.

ROMANS 6:14 NLT

When we taste the freedom of Christ's forgiveness, we enter into a new kind of relationship with our faults. They no longer dictate who we are or where we are going. We don't have to return to cycles that keep us locked in sin, shame, or fear. We can break free in the liberty of God's love! Now, when we sin, God mercifully offers us a fresh start every time.

As you continually yield your life to Christ, his grace leads you on a pathway that is filled with peace, love, and joy. Under his leadership, you go from glory to glory. Surely you will stumble, but God's Word promises that you will get up each time. Sin is no longer your master. Instead, you can lean on God's strength and walk forward in freedom. What glorious goodness you have to look forward to as you follow your gracious Redeemer!

Savior, thank you for setting me free from the grip of sin, fear, and death. Without you I would be lost. You are worthy of my praise, and I am dedicated to honoring you for all my days.

Law of Love

"This is My commandment, that you love one another,
just as I have loved you."

JOHN 15:12 NASB

Without Christ's sacrifice we would be slaves to the law.
We would be bound to a list of rules that none of us could
possibly fulfill. In Christ, we are set free from that kind of
life. Through his death and resurrection, Jesus fulfilled every
requirement of the law. He now calls us to faithfully follow
one rule. Everything we do should fall under the category of
loving each other as Christ has loved us.

As you get to know the character of Jesus, you will
further understand what it looks like to love others well.
Jesus taught with wisdom, and he communicated with
kindness. He laid his life down willingly. He noticed
the forgotten, broken, and overlooked. He was a perfect
reflection of the Father. If you are unsure how to love those
around you, look at his example of humility and servant-
hearted leadership.

*Jesus, I want to follow your example. Help me serve others with
kindness even when it is costly. Teach me how to lay my life
down willingly. I want to share your love with everyone I meet.*

All You Need

Through these he gave us the very great and precious
promises. With these gifts you can share in God's nature,
and the world will not ruin you with its evil desires.

2 PETER 1:4 NCV

We have everything we need to live and serve God.
Through our relationship with Christ, we are fully equipped
to do God's will. We can enjoy God's goodness and live
in a way that honors him. We all feel inadequate at times,
but it's important to remember that we don't rely on our
own strengths or weaknesses. Instead, we depend on God's
strength to get through the day. He is the one we truly need,
and Christ has given us full access to his presence.

You are blessed to share in God's nature. He generously
shares his perfection with all who follow him. As such,
nothing stands between you and the life that God intends
for you. Respond to his call and seek to honor him with
your actions. Fill your heart with truth and walk forward in
confidence, knowing that you are fully equipped to live a life
that pleases him.

*Lord, thank you for providing all I need to live and serve you.
You are so generous and wise. Keep my heart soft toward your
commands. I want to follow you faithfully all my days.*

FULLY KNOWN

You are all fair, my love,
And there is no spot in you.

SONG OF SOLOMON 4:7 NKJV

God loves each of us thoroughly. He is delighted by his creation. When he looks at us, he doesn't focus on our flaws. He sees what he made, and he calls us good. His love for us is great and unending. It's not that he can't see our imperfections, and so loves an inaccurate version of who we are. Rather, he sees us completely and loves us fully. He is aware of every strength and weakness, yet he loves us extravagantly.

While your flaws and mistakes might seem overwhelming to you, they are not to God. They don't get in the way or cause his love to diminish. While you are poignantly aware of what you lack, God is filled with delight when he looks at you. He loves every part of you. You can relax in his presence and enjoy his adoration.

Lord, I cannot comprehend your love. I am fully known and fully loved. I want to feel your delight and have confidence in how you see me.

WELL LOVED

You are so intimately aware of me, Lord.
You read my heart like an open book
and you know all the words I'm about to speak
before I even start a sentence!
You know every step I will take
before my journey even begins.

PSALM 139:3-4 TPT

The care of a loving parent is powerful. Confidence in
our parents' love gives us a firm foundation, and healthy
family connections provide a safe harbor for growth.
Whether or not we have experienced this kind of love in our
early years, we have a heavenly Father who loves us perfectly.
He wants us to know the security of his affection and the
sense of empowerment that comes from his love for us.

Just as a parent knows the tufts of their child's hair,
the shade of their eyes, or the shape of their hands, God is
intimately aware of you. He reads the pages of your heart
like an open book. He knows each of your thoughts, and
he sees the journey you will embark on. Nothing about you
surprises him!

*Father, you are my firm foundation. Your love is what keeps
me steady and secure. Thank you for knowing me fully and
loving me so well.*

HOPE FOR ETERNITY

He has made everything beautiful in its time. He has also
set eternity in the human heart; yet no one can fathom what
God has done from beginning to end.

ECCLESIASTES 3:11 NIV

No one can comprehend all that God has woven
together from the beginning of time. We see glimpses of
his creativity all around us, yet we won't see the full picture
until the end of this age. Deep in our hearts we know that
we are meant for more than what the world has to offer. This
sense of dissatisfaction comes from the fact that don't belong
in this world. We are meant for the perfection of God's
presence and the glory of our eternal home.

If you are frustrated and dissatisfied with your life, let
those feelings fan into flame anticipation for eternity. You
are not meant to be completely comfortable with the life
you have on earth. You were created for more than can be
found in this life. God, in his perfect wisdom, is leading you
on a path that ends in the great satisfaction of his eternal
presence. Look toward that day with a heart full of hope.

*Glorious God, I trust your timing and your faithfulness! I am
meant for eternal life with you. Fill me with anticipation for
Christ's return.*

Powerful Deliverance

The Lord their God will save them on that day
as the flock of his people;
For they are like jewels in a crown,
sparkling over his land.

ZECHARIAH 9:16 CSB

God's redemption is powerful. He not only saves us but also offers us peace. He has secured our position in his kingdom, settled our hearts, and showered us with affection. He does great and wonderful things for those who look to him for salvation. We were meant to thrive under the influence of his life-giving love. We can trust God to come through for us every time we need him. He is a powerful deliverer!

God desperately wants to redeem your life. Your journey with him doesn't end at salvation. He offers you so much more than just a place at the table. You are so loved by him. You have immense value, like a jewel in a crown. His desire for you is so much more than a position or a title. He wants to see you thrive. He wants to see you experience all the goodness and riches he has to offer.

Redeemer, thank you for redeeming me and giving me new life. Revive my heart with your love today. I want to experience more of your goodness.

One Thing

One thing have I asked of the LORD,
that will I seek after:
that I may dwell in the house of the LORD
all the days of my life,
to gaze upon the beauty of the LORD
and to inquire in his temple.

PSALM 27:4 ESV

We don't have to physically be in a house of worship to dwell with God. The Holy Spirit makes his home in each of us. God's presence is available to us at all times. There is nothing standing in our way. In any location, at any time of day, we can enjoy the richness of his presence. We can dwell on his beauty, and we can let his goodness wash over us.

God's presence is the absolute best place for you to be. If your aim is to live in the house of the Lord for all your days, you will be richly rewarded. He can meet every need you have, and he can fulfill every desire of your heart. As you gaze upon his beauty, your heart will find it's home with his. There is nothing better than dwelling in the house of the Lord.

Glorious God, your beauty is unmatched. I am undone by your great love. I am grateful that you are always close and accessible!

CORRECTION IS KIND

The LORD corrects those he loves,
just as a father corrects a child in whom he delights.

PROVERBS 3:12 NLT

Loving correction is an act of kindness. The truth will set us free. When we live within the confines of our mistakes, growth is limited. A loving parent, friend, or mentor shows us a better way. They pay attention to our actions and help us to grow in wisdom and maturity. We should be thankful for the people in our lives who love us enough to help us grow. The Lord's discipline should be viewed in the same manner.

God's discipline is evidence of his love. He knows what is best for you, and he doesn't want to see you miss his plans for your life. He cares immensely for you, and he is the perfect teacher and guide. Trust his leadership and lean into his correction. You can move forward in confidence, knowing that his discipline is good and perfect.

Father, I trust your wisdom and correction. Make my path straight and show me what needs to be corrected. I am open to your discipline because I trust your character.

Practical Love

No one has ever seen God; if we love one another,
God remains in us, and His love is perfected in us.

1 John 4:12 NASB

If we want to remain in God and for him to remain in
us, we must love his people. Love is the basis of his kingdom
and the foundation of every secure relationship. If we
want to love God well, we cannot neglect the call to love
others. There are endless ways to show God's love to those
around us. We can be mindful of our words, gracious with
others' mistakes, and eager to serve even when it costs us
something.

God's love is not conceptual. It is tangible and practical,
and it meets every need you have. Your love for others
should fall into those categories as well. There is an endless
list of how you can practically love others. Start with what
comes naturally to you. Do you like to bake, write, or do
yard work? You can drop off a meal, send an encouraging
note, or help someone with an outdoor project. Use your
gifts and talents to practically show love to those around you.

*Lord, thank you for the power of your love. Give me creative
ideas for loving the people in my life. I want my actions to
show them how much you love them.*

Spiritual Transformation

We can all draw close to him with the veil removed from our faces. And with no veil we all become like mirrors who brightly reflect the glory of the Lord Jesus. We are being transfigured into his very image as we move from one brighter level of glory to another.

2 Corinthians 3:18 tpt

We are shaped by what attracts our attention. Whether it's people, goals, or tangible objects, our mindsets are affected by what we focus on. If we want to be kinder, it is wise to spend time with kind people. If we want to be generous, surrounding ourselves with generous people can encourage us to open our hearts more. This also applies to our relationship with the Lord. The more time we spend with him, the more we will become like him.

When you look to the Lord, he will transform you. When you gaze at him in worship, his Spirit moves in you to make you more like him. The more you get to know his beautiful nature, the more you will apply it to your own life. If you want to be transformed by God, you must spend time with him. You need to know him in order to be like him.

God, thank you for your transformative power in my life. I want to be like you. Help me keep my eyes focused on you. I want your character to be the greatest influence in my life.

SPIRITUALLY MINDED

To be carnally minded is death,
but to be spiritually minded is life and peace.

ROMANS 8:6 NKJV

If we want to be spiritually minded, we must set our thoughts on things of the Spirit. It takes discipline that stems from grace to say no to the desires of our flesh. We all have propensities toward certain sins. By God's great mercy we are not slaves to any of our fleshly desires. Instead, we have been granted freedom and fortitude. We have been saved by grace, and we are equipped with everything we need to live in a way that honors God.

No matter what your particular battle looks like, you must first accept God's gift of grace. If your desire to please him comes from anything else, you will slide down the slippery slope of legalism. As you lean into his grace, he will lead you away from being carnally minded. As you spend time with him, he will renew your thoughts and give you peace.

Spirit, fill my mind and heart with truth. Help me dwell on what is pleasing and honoring to God. I don't want to be carnally minded, and I don't want to chase the desires of my flesh.

His Perspective

"You became famous among the nations, because you were so beautiful. Your beauty was perfect, because of the glory I gave you," says the Lord God.

EZEKIEL 16:14 NCV

Some of us have been told, either directly or indirectly, that we just don't meet the mark. We've believed the hurtful words of others; we've let them influence our thoughts and our actions. This is a travesty and is not what God intended for any of his children. He wants us to know how incredibly valuable we are. His desire is that we would know deep in our hearts that we are loved and cared for.

Have the words of others caused you to hide who you are? Maybe you've been told you're just too much, or not enough, or somehow both simultaneously. As God's creation, you are beautiful. You reflect his glory, and he is delighted by you. Take your hurt to him and let him carefully bandage each wound. Ask him what he thinks of you. As you seek to trust his opinion, he will give you the grace to believe it.

God, thank you for the power of your love. Thank you for reminding me of my identity. Help me elevate your perspective above all else.

ARISE AND SHINE

Arise, shine, for your light has come,
and the glory of the LORD shines over you.
For look, darkness will cover the earth,
and total darkness the peoples;
but the LORD will shine over you,
and his glory will appear over you.

ISAIAH 60:1-2 CSB

The Lord shines on his people. Even in the darkest valleys, the light of his presence shines on us. It lights the path, and it gives us confidence to move forward even when we don't know which direction we are going. With God on our side, we will never be overcome. No matter how dark the world becomes, we can confidently trust in God's abounding light.

God is familiar with the darkness of the world. He knows the trials you face. He is aware of the cultural, political, and social stress we are surrounded with. The good news is that no matter how dismal things may seem, God's light cannot be shrouded. His glory cannot be hidden, and his plans cannot be thwarted. Trust in his promises and move through each day with confidence. He is with, and you will not be overtaken.

Glorious God, shine your light on me. I want my life to reflect your glory. When I am tempted to despair in the darkness, give me confidence in your promises.

NOVEMBER

The LORD delights
in those who fear him,
who put their hope
in his unfailing love

PSALM 147:11 NIV

No Secrets

Even hell itself holds no secrets from the Lord God,
for before his eyes, all is exposed—
and so much more the heart of every human being.

PROVERBS 15:11 TPT

Everything is exposed before the Lord. He sees every situation and heart clearly. There is no such thing as secret sins or hidden motives. He cannot be tricked. We don't share our hearts with him because he is unaware. We share our hearts with him because it is good for us to remain soft and open to correction. He always knows the best way to lead us through any problem. He makes a way where we can't see one.

God knows your heart. This isn't meant to be intimidating or shame-inducing. There is safety and security in his omniscience. He does not use his knowledge to hold your sins against you or mockingly call out your weaknesses. His awareness provides you with a tower of refuge and strength in the fiercest storms.

God, I am so thankful that you know me better than I know myself. I trust you to hold me steady. I open my heart to you today. You see every part of me, and I am safe in your hands.

GOD WITHIN

God is within her, she will not fall;
God will help her at break of day.

PSALM 46:5 NIV

We are in God, and God is in us. When we submit ourselves to the law of his love and follow the ways of his kingdom, we can trust that he will keep us steady. He is our every present help in times of need. From the moment we wake in the morning, to the minute we lay our heads down at night, God is with us. His presence is a great blessing.

God is within you; you will not fall. He has made a covenant to redeem you, and he will not break his promise. Each new morning is an opportunity to know the mercy of God as it unfolds in your life. Even when people come against you, you can depend on the voice of the Lord. Even when unexpected trials arise, he will keep you safe in his presence.

Lord, I am yours, and you are mine. You have made your home in me, and I follow your voice. Continue to keep me, guide me, and teach me. With you on my side, I know I won't fail!

GENEROUS WISDOM

If any of you lacks wisdom, let him ask God, who gives
generously to all without reproach, and it will be given him.

JAMES 1:5 ESV

Whenever we recognize a weakness in ourselves, we
have an opportunity to depend on God's abundant strength.
We all lack wisdom in one way or another. Even the wisest
among us do not see everything clearly. In light of our lack,
we must resist pride. Pride stands in the way of humbly
receiving wisdom from God when we need it most. There
is freedom in admitting we are weak and seeking wisdom
straight from the source.

God will give you wisdom every time you ask for it. He
will give it generously and without bias. He will never turn
you away when you ask for help. He loves to teach and guide
his children. He is delighted when you turn to him. He will
direct your steps and lead you steadily on the right path. No
matter what you are lacking, God is capable of providing for
you in abundance. He will be faithful to meet your needs.

*God, thank you for the power of your wisdom. You see what I
need before I ask. Thank you for your abundant provision in
my life. I would be lost without you.*

BEFORE THEY CALL

"I will answer them before they even call to me.
While they are still talking about their needs,
I will go ahead and answer their prayers!"

ISAIAH 65:24 NLT

Before we form a prayer on our lips, God is already piecing our provisions together. He answers our prayers before we recognize our own needs. This is wonderful! Not only is God incredibly attentive to our needs, but he is also proactive in providing for us. He sees, and he is eager to help.

If you worry about how your needs will be met, today's verse is especially powerful. You can lay down each of your worries with intention and finality. The burdens you carry don't need to weigh you down. God knows exactly what plagues you. He knows what you need before you even attempt to tell him about it. Rest in his presence and trust in his faithfulness.

Father, I give you my worries, and I trust that you will help me. You see each of my days clearly. Help me rely on your faithfulness. Thank you for taking such good care of me.

Unmistakable Love

May the grace and joyous favor of the Lord Jesus Christ, the unambiguous love of God, and the precious communion that we share in the Holy Spirit be yours continually. Amen!

2 CORINTHIANS 13:14 TPT

God's love is unambiguous; it is clear as day. We cannot mistake it for anything other than what it is! The sun, even when it is hiding behind the clouds, is still obviously the sun. It is unmistakable. God's love is similar. It is steady, unchanging, and always reliable. The fruit of God's love is clear and abundant. It brings light, life, and hope.

Love is at the center of everything. You could wax on about God's love for all eternity and never scratch the surface of its power. May you know God's life-giving love in fresh ways today! May it fill your heart and overflow to those around you. God's desire is that you would experience the unending goodness found in receiving his love.

Lord, thank you for the power of your love that changes everything for me. I am not a slave to fear or shame. You have called me out of darkness and into the light. I am forever grateful for all you have done!

Heart Matters

The LORD said to Samuel, "Do not look at his appearance or at the height of his stature, because I have rejected him; for God does not see as man sees, since man looks at the outward appearance, but the LORD looks at the heart."

1 SAMUEL 16:7 NASB

While we tend to judge people based on appearances, God does not. He sees every part of us clearly. He looks beyond our actions and straight into our hearts. He understands our character and our intentions. This is what matters most to him. He doesn't care what we look like or how other people see us.

Surrender your heart to your gracious Father. Rely on his leadership and walk in his ways. May you feel his delight as you seek to live authentically before him. He knows you thoroughly, and he loves you abundantly. You don't have to impress him, and you don't have to strive to look a certain way. Your heart matters most, and God sees it clearly.

Dear Lord, may my heart be a beautiful offering to you. You see every part of me, and I am thankful for your perspective. Transform me into your likeness and help me honor you with my life.

Unchanging One

"They will be changed like clothes,
and you will fold them up and put them away.
But you are 'I AM.'
You never change, years without end!"

Hebrews 1:12 tpt

Though the world is ever-changing, God remains constant. Everything in nature has a beginning and an end. The cycle of life repeats all around us. Seasons come and go. Life shifts, trials come, and little is constant. Change is inevitable, except when it comes to God. God never changes. Every part of his character is steady. His plans will never shift, and he never changes his mind.

Throughout the ages, God has remained the same. He is steadfast, loyal, and merciful. Praise God, for he is better than you can imagine. His love endures forever! It is never too late to receive the love he offers you. No matter where you are in life, you haven't run out of time. If you have breath in your lungs, his enduring love is available to you.

God, envelop me in your unchanging love. I am thankful that you remain steady and constant. I rely on you for all I need. I trust you and turn my heart toward you.

Way Maker

You made a way through the sea
and paths through the deep waters,
but your footprints were not seen.

PSALM 77:19 NCV

Natural barriers cannot deter the Lord's plans. He separated the Red Sea so his people could escape captivity in Egypt. They walked across dry land and rejoiced on the other side. He gave his people fresh water out of a rock in the desert. He fed them bread from heaven each morning. He miraculously provided for their needs every step of the way.

There may be situations in your life that look impossible. Maybe you can't see a way out of a problem. Maybe the solution is out of reach and beyond your grasp. Turn your eyes toward the Lord. He is capable of making a way where there isn't one. He is not bound by the same limitations as you. Will you trust him as he guides you? He will not abandon you, not even for a moment. He is faithful, and he is capable of rescuing you.

Miraculous One, you are the God of miracles. Move in my life and help me trust in your faithfulness. Make a path where I cannot see one. Lead me where you want me to go.

LOVE'S DESIRE

I am my love's,
and his desire is for me.

SONG OF SONGS 7:10 CSB

There are many kinds of love, but the deepest is the love God has for us. It encompasses every kind of passion and affection. It is given freely with no strings attached. It is consistent, safe, kind, and perfect. God's love for his creation is abundant and wonderful. It brings him great joy to shower his affection on all he made.

God loves you more than you can imagine. At your worst, and at your best, you delight God. It doesn't matter how you look or feel. It doesn't matter how many times you've failed or succeeded. God's desire is for you. He sees you as valuable, precious, and worth pursuing. He loves you fully and completely. Today, receive his love and let it fill every corner of your heart.

God, I don't want to resist your love. I am so thankful to be yours. Thank you for loving me and calling me your own. Give me a fresh revelation of your love for me.

Power and Insight

"Counsel and sound judgment are mine;
I have insight, I have power."

PROVERBS 8:14 NIV

The book of Proverbs is all about wisdom. One of the most consistent themes is that God is the holder of all wisdom, and he is eager to share it with all who ask. Every treasure of wisdom and knowledge is hidden in him. There is no other source of wisdom that holds a candle to God. There is nothing else worth seeking. He is the living expression of wisdom!

In God, all of your needs are fulfilled. He has the wisdom you need. He sees each of your days clearly, and he knows precisely how to lead you through any problem you face. There is nothing beyond God's understanding. He has a limitless supply of insight and power. No matter what you are dealing with, he knows the solution. Go to him confidently and trust that he will give you the wisdom you need.

God, you said those who ask will receive, and those who seek will find. I need your wisdom. I don't want to depend on my limited understanding. Give me insight and lead me toward truth today!

SEEK WISDOM

The unfolding of your words gives light;
it imparts understanding to the simple.

PSALM 119:130 ESV

When we open our hearts to the Lord, he unfolds his wisdom for us. He does not hide his ways from those who seek him. If we find ourselves confused and not knowing which way to turn, our best counsel rests with the Holy Spirit. He guides us and points us toward the power of God's Word.

Scripture is always available to you. You may have prioritized studying the Word, or it may be an untapped resource in your life. Either way, its value remains the same. God's truth never changes. No matter what you are facing, understanding can be found by seeking God. He is delighted when you ask him for help. Talk to him, read his Word, and trust his guidance.

Lord, unfold your truth before me. I seek your understanding and guidance. You are able to lead me through whatever I face today. I rely on you and your wisdom.

Highest Calling

Owe nothing to anyone—except for your obligation to love one another. If you love your neighbor, you will fulfill the requirements of God's law.

ROMANS 13:8 NLT

When we live in the light of God's love, we can't keep it to ourselves. Our only obligation to each other is to love one another as God has loved us. No other instruction is as important as this. The rules we follow might make us feel successful, but they mean nothing compared to our calling to love each other well. It's not easy to serve and lay our lives down for others, but it is the only thing that has eternal value.

May each of your choices be motivated by love. Worldly success means nothing compared to the great value of loving others. If your priorities are out of order, ask God to help you rearrange them. He will guide you gently and help you move forward. Everyone gets distracted from what really matters. Even if you have to do it over and over, turn your attention toward your highest calling. Follow Christ's example and share God's love with those around you.

Lord Jesus, I want to walk in the power of your love! Help me share your love with everyone I encounter. I want to follow your example. Give me creative ideas for loving others.

Look Beyond

We fix our eyes not on what is seen, but on what is unseen, since what is seen is temporary, but what is unseen is eternal.

2 Corinthians 4:18 niv

Every day we face new challenges. There are times we are prepared for trials, and at other times we are blindsided by them. Whether we feel like we are in control or not, we must remember that there is more to life than what we observe. We are not meant to focus on the details of this life. Instead, Scripture reminds us to set our eyes upon what is unseen. We are meant to keep our eyes turned toward the eternal life God offers.

When you focus on the things that last, your heart will remain rooted in everlasting hope. When you have the right perspective, you won't be swayed by the trials of this life. Your faith will remain steadfast because you are confident in the goodness God has in store for you. It's hard to focus on what can't be seen, but the Holy Spirit empowers you to do it. He will help you fix your eyes on what really matters.

Everlasting God, fill me with new hope. Help me see beyond the details of my life. Help me look past what is temporary and focus on eternity with you.

Faithful Messiah

"To give light to those who sit
in darkness and the shadow of death,
To guide our feet into the way of peace."

LUKE 1:79 NKJV

Prophets foretold the great things Jesus would do before he ever walked the earth. He is the long-awaited Messiah. For hundreds of years, God's people eagerly waited for their promised redemption. They knew that God would make a way where there wasn't one. Christ's birth, life, death, and resurrection fulfilled every prophecy made about him. God faithfully worked out his plan just like he said he would. Through Christ, God made a way.

Though this world is dark, Jesus is your light. Even if your life doesn't look how you expected, Jesus is your peace. He remains constant and true, never leaving you to walk through your troubles alone. You aren't waiting for redemption. It has already come! No matter what your life looks like, your hope is anchored in Christ. The Messiah came once, and he will surely come again.

Messiah, you are worth waiting for. I rely on your faithfulness. Thank you for redeeming me. I eagerly wait for you to come back and make all things right.

Cascading Mercy

May God's mercy, peace, and love cascade over you!

JUDE 1:2 TPT

God's mercy, peace, and love are unlimited. He has an abundance of all of them. We are called to posture ourselves under the waterfall of his goodness. As his presence washes over us, we receive the peace he offers. If we trust him, we will see that he has good things in store for us. When we are with him, we get to experience the depth of his love for us.

God's mercies are new every single morning. His peace is present even in the fiercest storm. His love is faithful and consistent. In God's presence, you are safe and secure. If you are overwhelmed today, may God's mercy, peace, and love cascade over you. Let the Lord tend to your soul as you lean into his goodness. Seek him, open your heart to him, and he will take care of you.

Merciful God, you are so abundant in goodness. I want to experience more of your mercy, peace, and love. I give you all my fears, questions, shortcomings, and needs. Thank you for the gift of your presence.

Confidence and Strength

Those who respect the LORD will have security,
and their children will be protected.

PROVERBS 14:26 NCV

When we live in awe of the Lord, we honor him.
To be in awe of God, we must recognize how great he is
and how much we lack. Humility leads to reverence, and
reverence leads to devotion. Devotion then leads to a life
fully surrendered to the Lord. This is our greatest security.
Knowing that our life is in God's hands allows us to live in
true freedom. God is our confidence and our strength no
matter what trouble we face.

When you devote your life to God, even your children
will reap the benefits. God is always faithful to his people.
Generation after generation will be blessed. As you embrace
your need for redemption, you open yourself up to every
blessing God has in store for you. He wants you and your
children after you, to experience the goodness of his
presence and the promise of eternal life.

*God, I want to grow in respect and awe for you. Help me be
aware of my need for you. I don't want to rely on my own
strength. You are my security and my protection.*

Extremely Gracious

The LORD is gracious and compassionate,
slow to anger and great in faithful love.

PSALM 145:8 CSB

God is slow to anger. This statement is true and without exception. It doesn't say he is slow to anger unless we really mess up. He isn't slow to anger unless provoked in a certain way. God is slow to anger all the time. We can rely on this aspect of his character. We can confidently approach him with our greatest failures because his reactions are not like ours. He is not disappointed or waiting to unleash his rage upon us.

God is not angry with you. He does not look at you with a list of your failures in his hand. He won't draw you into his presence just so he can make sure you know how you can improve. His main directive is not to make you into a better person. God wants good things for you because he loves you. He cares for you deeply, and he wants to see you thrive in the abundance of his blessings. He is kind and gracious toward you even when you don't deserve it.

Gracious God, thank you for being slow to anger. Help me see your character rightly. At times I've seen you as angry or domineering. Change my perspective and show me how gentle you are.

So Much Better

"My thoughts are not your thoughts,
neither are your ways my ways,"
declares the LORD.

ISAIAH 55:8 NIV

How often do we ascribe our own thoughts and feelings to others? We make assumptions that whatever matters to us must also matter to them. We go through mental gymnastics trying to understand why someone behaves in a certain way. Not only do we jump to conclusions with people, but we do the same thing with God. We take our understanding and unconsciously apply it to his way of thinking.

God's thoughts are not like yours. His ways are higher than your ways. His motives are always right, and his understanding is always unbiased. God's ways are always in line with his character. His actions aren't tainted by his faults like yours might be. This is why he is so trustworthy and reliable. Everything he does is perfect, and you can depend on him. Instead of trying to navigate your day alone, lean on the Lord.

Lord, you do all things perfectly. Your ways are better than mine, and your thoughts are higher than mine. I surrender to you today. I trust you to lead me well.

First and Last

"Who has performed and done this,
calling the generations from the beginning?
I, the Lord, the first,
and with the last; I am he."

ISAIAH 41:4 ESV

God was at the beginning of all things, and he will be at the end. He will stay with his people every step of the way. He created us with love and has faithfully provided us with a path to redemption. In his mercy, he has reconciled us to himself. He could have left us to bear the weight of our sin, but instead, he saved us. He is the God of restoration!

God has done great things for you. Even on days when you can't see him in the details of your life, you can testify that he has redeemed you. Even when he doesn't answer prayers how you expect, you can rejoice in your salvation. Sometimes, the circumstances of our lives cause us to praise him, and sometimes, you must look beyond your circumstances and praise him for what cannot be seen. He will be faithful from beginning to end, no matter what it looks like in between.

Everlasting God, I choose to follow you no matter where you take me. Your plans are better than my own, and your wisdom is more complete than my understanding. I trust in your faithfulness.

ALLY AND FRIEND

The eyes of the LORD watch over those who do right;
his ears are open to their cries for help.

PSALM 34:15 NLT

When we align ourselves with God, we gain salvation
and full redemption. We also gain the most incredible ally and
friend. Through submission to Christ, we secure an eternal
position in God's family. Our future inheritance is unshakeable,
and he is also our ever-present help while we walk the earth.
He does not leave us to navigate life on our own.

God is mindful of eternity, and he is mindful of each of
your days. His ears are turned toward you. There is no such
thing as an insignificant detail to God. He sees every part of
your life, and he wants to walk with you through all of it. As
you seek to do his will, he promises to be with you every step
of the way. He watches over you, and he answers your cries.

*Lord, as I follow you, watch over me. Keep me safe and lead
me according to your will. I trust your guidance, and I am
thankful for your attentiveness.*

Children of Light

You, brothers and sisters, are not in darkness, so that the day
would overtake you like a thief; for you are all sons of light
and sons of day. We are not of night nor of darkness; so then
let's not sleep as others do, but let's be alert and sober.

1 Thessalonians 5:4-6 nasb

In Christ, we have been welcomed into the family of
God. We are children of the light. We don't hide in shadows
with our faces covered in shame. We have been liberated and
set free for all eternity. We don't get distracted by the ways of
the world, and we don't despair when trials come our way.
Instead, we keep our eyes securely focused on the eternal
glory that is to come.

When you live in the light of God's truth, you have a
sense of security and safety. You are not caught off guard
or surprised by trials because your eyes are wide open. You
will encounter suffering, but you will not face it alone. You
will face temptation, but you have been equipped to stand
strong. As a child of light, you have everything you need to
persevere until the end.

*Father, thank you for shining your light on me. Keep me
steady as I follow you. Help me be alert and sober-minded as I
wait for Jesus to come back.*

ABUNDANT LIFE

When you live a life of abandoned love,
surrendered before the awe of God,
here's what you'll experience:
Abundant life. Continual protection.
And complete satisfaction!

PROVERBS 19:23 TPT

Today's verse is full of incredible promises. Do we need any other reasons to follow, love, or worship him? There is goodness beyond measure in his kingdom. There is safety and peace in his presence. There is satisfaction for our souls that no one can take away. God's promises are great, and he will fulfill all of them. His plans are more wonderful than we can imagine.

Everything you are looking for is found in God. He is the only one who can satisfy the deepest longings of your soul. He offers you true freedom and abundant life. He protects you even when you don't see a threat of danger. He sustains you even when you think you are the one in control. He surrounds you with his love, and he provides for your needs. Praise God today because he is worthy of being worshipped.

God, you are full of wonderful mercy. Thank you for everything you've done for me. My life is full of goodness because of you, and I am so proud to be yours.

GUIDED BY GOD

You will guide me with Your counsel,
And afterward receive me to glory.

PSALM 73:24 NKJV

God's wise counsel is offered to all who yield to his leadership. He is not stingy with his advice, and he does not withhold knowledge. When we seek him, he hears our cries and answers us. He gives us grace to understand his ways and equips us to follow his instructions. All we need is found in him, our one true source.

God is not too busy to lead you. He delights in doing so and is joyful when you look to him for counsel. He will not shame you for not knowing how to move forward. He doesn't count your need for him as a weakness or failure. Dependence on God is a sign of strength and maturity. It shows that you are aware of both your humanity and his greatness.

God, you are my guide, friend, and teacher. You are my shepherd and my shelter. I trust you to guide me through each day of my life. There is no one better equipped to help me with whatever I am facing.

Enduring Love

Even much water cannot put out the flame of love;
floods cannot drown love.
If a man offered everything in his house for love,
people would totally reject it.

SONG OF SOLOMON 8:7 NCV

God's love cannot be tamed, overcome, extinguished, or diminished. It is fierce, and it will remain that way forever. It is not foolish to be consumed by the fire of God's love. As it overtakes our fears, doubts, and shame, we realize that yielding to God's love is less like a sacrifice and more of a delight.

Love is always worth it! The love of God may lead you to places you would never go on your own, but you can trust that God sees your path clearly. Even though the steps may seem unclear to you, you can have confidence in God's purpose for your life. When you allow God's love to be the foundation for every choice you make, you will find that your steps are steady and secure. His enduring love is your greatest gift.

Lord, please surround me and fill me with your love. I surrender to your plans. Thank you for the blessing of your presence and the enduring faithfulness of your love.

Abundant Grace

The grace of our Lord was poured out on me abundantly,
along with the faith and love that are in Christ Jesus.

1 TIMOTHY 1:14 NIV

There is an endless flow of empowering strength in
God's presence. He gives us all we need to grow in faith and
love. He compensates for our weaknesses, and he encourages
us when we are weary. God equips us to persevere through
every trial we face. He doesn't leave us to figure it out on our
own. He pours out his grace even though it is undeserved.

It doesn't matter what you've done in the past or how
many times you've failed. God strengthens your weaknesses
and gives you what you need. When you repent of your sins,
God's grace allows you to move forward. It equips you to be
transformed into his likeness. Only from a place of abundant
grace can you live in a God-honoring way without being
bound to legalism. When you rely on grace, there is no room
for pride, boasting, or striving.

*God, thank you for the gift of salvation. Thank you for the
grace you've poured out on me. I devote my life to you. Help
me honor you with my actions.*

Forever Good

Give thanks to the LORD, for he is good.
His love endures forever.

PSALM 136:1 NIV

The goodness of God is never-ending. We can't measure it or use it up. If we pay attention, we will see glimpses of God's goodness everywhere. It can be found in every aspect of creation. Taking note of his blessings, big and small, can keep your heart soft. The more you praise God for all he's done, the more your heart will be filled with thanksgiving.

Today, deliberately observe God's goodness in the world around you. Intentionally look for the blessings he has showered you with. It might take a bit of mental discipline, but this practice will draw you closer to God. Let your delight in creation lead you to greater delight in your Creator. Every good gift comes from his hands, and he is worthy of all your praise.

God, you are forever kind, gracious, and beautiful. Open my eyes to expressions of your goodness in the world around me. I will hunt for them like treasures!

Unshakeable Kingdom

Let us be grateful for receiving a kingdom that cannot be shaken, and thus let us offer to God acceptable worship, with reverence and awe.

HEBREWS 12:28 ESV

The kingdom of God will not crumble or fall. It does not operate like the worldly ones we've seen. Nations and governments rise and fall all the time. History is riddled with accounts of different rulers gaining and losing their domain. God's kingdom is eternal. There will never be a story told of its collapse. It is secure and unshakeable.

God's kingdom is established, and you don't have to be concerned about its stability. His plans will succeed; he will keep every promise he's made. No matter how many disappointments you face, you can have faith in God's plans. You will spend eternity enjoying the full goodness of his presence. Let anticipation for that day fill you with hope and allow you to persevere until the end.

Mighty King, I put my faith in your plans. I trust you to do what you say. Your Word is reliable, and I look forward to seeing your promises fulfilled. Help me persevere until I'm with you forever.

Looking Down

God looks down from heaven
on the entire human race;
he looks to see if anyone is truly wise,
if anyone seeks God.

PSALM 53:2 NLT

God looks from heaven to see who is searching for him. He doesn't stare down like a tyrant looking for flaws. He is like an attentive father who keeps an eye out for his child coming down the driveway. He waits eagerly for each of us to turn toward him. Those who seek God will find him. He is always ready to meet us when we look for him.

God is not hiding from you. He is not far away, and he is not giving you the silent treatment. Scripture is clear that when you look for him, you will find him. When you knock, the door will be opened. Trust that his Word is true. Fill your heart with his promises and ask him to meet you. He will show up, and he will continue to move in your life.

Father, I reach out to you today. I want to be close to you. When I feel alone or forgotten, remind me you are close. Strengthen my faith and remind me of your promises.

At His Table

"I confer on you a kingdom, just as my Father conferred one on me, so that you may eat and drink at my table in my kingdom and sit on thrones, judging the twelve tribes of Israel."

LUKE 22:29-30 NIV

All who come to Jesus and follow his ways are welcomed into his kingdom. We don't have to fight for a place at the table of our King. Scripture tells us that all will be equal in the kingdom of heaven. All who come to celebrate will feast with him. We need only to accept his invitation and faithfully follow him.

You will never have to prove yourself to God. When you surrendered your life to Christ you became an heir in his kingdom. You don't have to convince him of your worth or defend your position. You don't need to worry about imposter syndrome or question if you belong. As an heir, everything God has is available to you. It is his delight to share it with you.

Jesus, give me grace to quit striving. I want to be confident in my position within your kingdom. Help me remember I am a beloved child and an heir. Thank you for the eternal security I've found in you.

MIRACLE AFTER MIRACLE

Let them give thanks to the LORD for his love
and for the miracles he does for people.
He satisfies the thirsty
and fills up the hungry.

PSALM 107:8-9 NCV

There are so many reasons to be grateful to God. We can
be thankful for the food on our tables and the clean water we
have to drink. We can be thankful for the close relationships
we have with our loved ones and the stability of a paycheck.
We can rejoice over our health and the ability to watch a
beautiful sunset. Our gratitude could go on forever. God has
done great things for each of us.

Your life is full of miracles. From your birth until now,
God has been at work. He is the reason for every good thing
you've experienced. He satisfies you when you are thirsty,
and he fills you when you are hungry. He sustains your life,
and he faithfully provides for you. When you turn to him, he
helps you every time. Give him credit where it is due! God's
care for you is precise and perfect.

*Marvelous One, you move in miraculous ways, and I'm so
grateful to be yours. Show me how you've been faithful to
care for me. You have been so good to me. I praise you for all
you've done.*

December

God shows his love for us
in that while we were still sinners,
Christ died for us.

ROMANS 5:8 ESV

He Lights the Path

You will light my lamp;
The LORD my God will enlighten my darkness.

PSALM 18:28 NKJV

There is no darkness that God cannot enlighten. He reveals what is hidden and helps us navigate when we cannot see. We can trust his guidance because his perspective is so much greater than ours. In any given situation, we are prone to bias and can't see the whole picture clearly. God sees what we cannot. He understands every aspect and nuance.

No matter what type of conflict you are facing, God can shine his light on it. Maybe you're wrestling with something internally and are unsure how to move forward; God can guide you. Maybe you're in a difficult situation with a friend and are struggling to find a resolution; God can guide you. No matter what the details are, he can bring light to the darkness. He can make a way where you cannot see one.

God, I rely on you when I don't know what to do. I trust your judgment and ability to navigate my problems. Make a way when I am lost. Shine your light in the darkness and lead me through the trials I am facing.

MASTER CRAFTER

He called him Lord, saying,
"Lord, you formed the earth in the beginning
and with your own hands you crafted the cosmos."

HEBREWS 1:10 TPT

God's ability and resources are unlimited. He spoke the universe into existence, and he breathed life into all creatures. He is the One who formed it all. It's incredible that we can have daily communion with the creator of all things. His power is beyond our understanding, yet we are his greatest delight. We are the work of his hands, and he is pleased with what he's done.

Do you realize how God feels about you? He has the ability to create whatever he wants. He does not have limits, and he is not bound by the expectations of others. He does exactly what he wants, and his deeds are always perfect. From that place of perfection, he created you. He made you intentionally and with love.

Creator, I am in awe of who you are and all you do. Help me see myself the way you do. You are pleased with your creation, and I want to honor you.

Follow His Way

Make your ways known to me, LORD;
teach me your paths.

PSALM 25:4 CSB

The paths of the Lord are life-giving and true. They are full of light, wisdom, and peace. This doesn't mean we won't face trials or forks in the road, but we can know the peace of God in the midst of them. When we seek God and desire to follow his ways, he will guide our steps. He will give us confidence, and he will equip us to do his will.

God's will for your life is not complicated. It's not an unsolvable mystery. There is no need to lose sleep over it or have anxiety about accomplishing it. First and foremost, his desire for you is to love him and others with all your heart. If you spend all your days focused on that, you'll be on the right path. The circumstances of your life are far less important than your proximity to God. Trust him with each step you take, and he will lead you closer to his heart.

Faithful Lord, help me follow you faithfully. I want each step I take to lead me closer to you. Teach me your ways and guide me in truth. I want to honor you all of my days.

EVERY MORNING

Let the morning bring me word of your unfailing love,
for I have put my trust in you.
Show me the way I should go,
for to you I entrust my life.

PSALM 143:8 NIV

Every morning is a new opportunity to experience
God's miraculous love. His mercies are fresh and present.
We can count on his enduring love to meet us at the dawn of
each new day. He is as faithful as the rising sun. Even after
the darkest night, we can trust that the light will come again.
He fills us with fresh hope, and he gives us what we need to
live a life that honors him.

Today is a fresh start for you. No matter what yesterday
looked like, you can be sure that God's unfailing love rises
up to greet you. He already knows how your day will unfold.
Look to him for direction and guidance. Allow him to equip
you for whatever you might face. Praise him for sustaining
you and giving you the opportunity to wake up and serve
him again.

*Lord, thank you for your faithfulness. I need your gracious
power in my life, and I'm so grateful to know that you are
with me every step of the way. I surrender to your leadership,
and I trust you to guide me today!*

Powerful Sacrifice

Have this mind among yourselves, which is yours in Christ Jesus, who, though he was in the form of God, did not count equality with God a thing to be grasped, but emptied himself, by taking the form of a servant, being born in the likeness of men.

PHILIPPIANS 2:5-7 ESV

Jesus Christ is the Son of God, yet he displayed perfect humility. When he walked the earth, he didn't flaunt his title or demand special treatment. Even though it would have made sense given his status, he didn't expect others to serve him. Instead, he laid his life down. He spent his time teaching and sharing about God's kingdom. He loved others when it was inconvenient for him, and he faithfully did what the Father asked of him.

If you want to follow Jesus, serving others must be a top priority. This may look different for everyone, but the attitude is the same. A heart that is yielded to Jesus looks for ways to love others even when it costs something. Like Jesus, you are called to humbly put the needs of others before your own. Today, remember that God will provide for you, and you are free to generously love those around you.

Lord Jesus, thank you for the power of your sacrifice. I want to follow your example of servant hearted leadership. Help me be more like you.

WOVEN TOGETHER

I want them to be encouraged and knit together by strong ties of love. I want them to have complete confidence that they understand God's mysterious plan, which is Christ himself.

COLOSSIANS 2:2 NLT

We are all connected by a common thread of love. Through Christ, we are woven together into a family that goes beyond blood or genetics. Though we come from different backgrounds, speak different languages, and have different preferences and personalities, God's love remains the constant tie that holds us together. Instead of focusing on what divides us, we should focus on what brings us together.

It can be tempting to let divisive issues cause separation within the body of Christ. It's normal to want to be around people who think and act like you. It feels comfortable and easy when your relationships don't challenge the way you act or think. Remember that God's love which knits everyone together is stronger and more important than individual opinions. While you may have preferences, don't elevate them above your calling to love well. Let God soften your heart and equip you to love as he does.

Lord Jesus, I don't want my opinions to override my ability to graciously love those around me. Soften my heart and give me your perspective. Teach me how to love like you do.

EMOTIONAL SECURITY

Evening and morning and at noon,
I will complain and moan,
And He will hear my voice.

PSALM 55:17 NASB

God is so gracious that he even hears our moaning and complaining. He is such a patient Father! We don't have to present ourselves perfectly or deal with our bad attitudes before we approach him. He can manage our honest and raw emotions. We don't have to worry about offending him or hurting his feelings. He is delighted when we turn to him and give him space to move in our lives.

As God's child, you can experience great emotional security. No matter how you feel, God hears you and loves you. There is no part of you that is too overwhelming for him. You are not too much. Let him decipher your confusing thoughts. Let him carry the burdens you don't know what to do with. He will untangle your messy emotions if you let him.

Father, thank you for listening to me no matter how I present myself. I surrender my emotions to you. Help me sort through my thoughts and teach me how to glorify you. Thank you for being so gentle and kind.

CREATIVE INSPIRATION

And through his creative inspiration
this Living Expression made all things,
for nothing has existence apart from him!

JOHN 1:3 TPT

God is full of creative inspiration. Look at how he has woven creation together perfectly. Each part has a purpose. Entire systems and processes are at work that we can't even see. If he can sustain the entire universe, surely, he can manage our problems. When we are stuck, he has the insight we need. He always has solutions for our problems. He is never at a loss for what to do or where to go.

Don't hesitate to trust God's creativity. It's easy to get so caught up in the flow of life that you forget the resources that are available to you. There is divine inspiration for every problem you face. You simply need to ask. He wants to be part of the details of your life. God has everything you need and more. Invite him into your day and allow him to lead you each step of the way. Rely on his leadership and trust his expertise.

Lord Jesus, guide me with your perfect wisdom. Give me your insight and help me solve problems the way you would. Your ways are higher than mine, and I trust your guidance.

Do No Harm

Love does no harm to a neighbor;
therefore love is the fulfillment of the law.

ROMANS 13:10 NKJV

When we meditate on love as it is described in Scripture, we can always point it back to God. Since God is love, we can interchange his name with the term itself. Love does no harm to a neighbor because God does no harm to a neighbor. We are meant to follow his example. Instead of being bound by the requirements of the law, we are free to love as God loves. Loving others is our highest calling.

What does it look like to do no harm? When you deliberately seek to encourage, help, and build others up, you honor God's definition of love. When you miss the mark, you can humbly admit your wrongdoing and move forward. Loving others is not meant to be another rule you must follow perfectly. Relax, ask God for help, and he will gently lead you in the way of love. He will help you build bridges and strengthen relationships.

God, thank you that I am not bound to the law. Help me love as you have loved me. I don't want to harm my neighbor. Show me ways to lift others up and point them to you.

Unexpected Goodness

The angel said to them, "Do not be afraid. I am bringing you
good news that will be a great joy to all the people. Today your
Savior was born in the town of David. He is Christ, the Lord."

LUKE 2:10-11 NCV

Good news is not always obvious in the moment it first
appears. When the angel appeared before the shepherds near
Bethlehem, they were terrified. They were out in the middle
of their fields at night and were suddenly surrounded by
glorious light. It was as if the angel came out of nowhere. It was
unexpected and unplanned yet ended up being a great blessing.
Sometimes, this is how God chooses to move in our lives.

God is never surprised. When unexpected things
happen in your life, he is not taken aback. He is acutely
aware of each detail even when you are taken off guard.
Especially if you're someone who loves a concise plan,
remember to be open to the unexpected work of God.
Loosen up your grip and leave space in your life for him to
move in ways that don't make sense to you. If your eyes are
on him, you will not be disappointed.

*Glorious One, bring peace to my heart when I am surprised.
Speak to me directly through your Spirit. I trust that you have
good things in store for me even when they are unexpected.*

Kingdom Inheritance

"Then the King will say to those on his right, 'Come, you
who are blessed by my Father; inherit the kingdom prepared
for you from the foundation of the world.'"

MATTHEW 25:34 CSB

All those who come to the Father through Christ have
his eternal kingdom as their inheritance. While we walk this
earth, we are part of his kingdom, but one day, we will share
in its fullness. We will live forever in the perfection of God's
presence. There will be no more suffering, pain, or tears. We
look forward to this glorious reality, and in the meantime,
we trust God to faithfully lead us toward it.

You have so much to look forward to! No matter what
your circumstances are, one day you will delight in the joy of
eternal life. You will see all God's plans clearly and you will
not lack anything. Your understanding will be complete, and
you will rejoice with every other believer in the presence of
your King. May your anticipation for that day motivate you
to persevere through the trials of this life.

*Faithful One, your plans and promises are great. I cannot
wait to spend eternity with you. Thank you for saving me and
making me an heir to your kingdom. Help me stay faithful as I
wait for Christ's return.*

Joyous Freedom

As God's loving servants, you live in joyous freedom from
the power of sin. So consider the benefits you now enjoy—
you are brought deeper into the experience of true holiness
that ends with eternal life!

ROMANS 6:22 TPT

When we spend our lives yielded to God's love, we
have joyous freedom over sin. Fear no longer holds us back,
and shame has no power over our choices. We are free to
glorify God in all we do. He has fully equipped us with
abundant grace to live pleasing and fruitful lives. As servants
of the living God, we do what he asks of us because he is
trustworthy, and his mercy never fails.

When you trust Jesus for the salvation of your soul, he
fills you with grace. God now sees you with eyes of mercy,
and you receive an inheritance of eternal life. The Holy
Spirit equips you to honor God with your choices. You have
everything you need. There is nothing standing between
you and the abundant life Christ paid for. Remember that he
has overcome every obstacle for you. If shame threatens to
overtake you, or you feel incapable of managing your flesh,
put your trust in Christ's ability to handle your sins.

*Father, I am so grateful for the freedom you have given me!
You have liberated me and given me victory over sin.*

OVERWHELMING GOODNESS

The Spirit of the Lord GOD is upon me,
because the LORD has anointed me
to bring good news to the poor;
he has sent me to bind up the brokenhearted,
to proclaim liberty to the captives,
and the opening of the prison to those who are bound.

ISAIAH 61:1 ESV

The Spirit of the Lord rested on Jesus and gave him the power to do great things when he walked the earth. His actions were evidence of God's overwhelming goodness. Each declaration made in Isaiah still applies today. Because of Jesus and his sacrifice, there is good news for the poor and brokenhearted. He is still liberating the captives and bringing freedom to the imprisoned among us.

Rejoice today because of everything Jesus has done for you. How has he set you free? What would your life be like without him? Take note of his great faithfulness and praise him for the unique way he has saved you. Everyone's story is different, but we have all been delivered from the power of sin and death. No matter the details of your testimony, Jesus is worthy of your praise and devotion.

Jesus, I am so thankful for you. Thank you for the hope, freedom, and joy you have given me. Without you and your sacrifice, I would be lost and helpless.

Safe Forever

You have not handed me over to my enemies
but have set me in a safe place.

PSALM 31:8 NLT

If we are walking in the light of God's love, we do not
need to fear. Even when our physical circumstances feel
unsafe, we know that our spirit is secure with him. There
is no force in the universe that can remove us from his
hands. Though certain situations look hopeless from our
perspective, we know that God sees everything clearly. He
will faithfully keep his promises. No matter what happens in
this life, there will be eternal safety and belonging in eternity.

God promises to keep you safe. He watches over you,
and he protects you when you aren't even aware of danger.
He sustains your life, and he renews your spirit each day as
you rely on him. When you feel discouraged, or can't see
God's hand in your life, remember that your perspective isn't
always complete. He is moving whether you see it or not.
Even when it's hard, trust that God is holding you steady.

*Lord, you are my hiding place when I have nowhere to run. You
are my shelter, and you keep me safe. I trust you to keep your
promises. Hold me close and keep me steady as I follow you.*

REST WELL

The one who has entered His rest has himself also rested
from his works, as God did from His.

HEBREWS 4:10 NASB

God set an example for us when he rested after
creating the universe. The Sabbath was instituted to place
parameters for rest into the lives of God's people. It is good
and necessary for us to rest. There is endless work; we will
always find more to do. Instead of being focused on our own
success, it's important to follow God's standard. If he has
declared that rest is needed, we are wise to listen.

Engaging in true rest is often countercultural. For some,
rest means taking a day off and setting the to-do list aside.
For others, it might mean turning off the phone and taking
a break from constant communication. The definition of rest
in your life is between you and God. Ask the Holy Spirit to
lead you to rest. Pray about the practical application of rest,
and then faithfully incorporate those patterns into the way
you live.

*Creator, I want to build rhythms of rest into my life. Give me
creative ideas and help me execute them. As I seek to honor
you, refresh my body, mind, and spirit.*

New Life

The desert and the parched land will be glad;
    the wilderness will rejoice and blossom.
Like the crocus, it will burst into bloom;
    it will rejoice greatly and shout for joy.

ISAIAH 35:1-2 NIV

God's redemption brings new life. Deserts become gardens, and desolate wilderness blooms abundantly. We have all known seasons of suffering; we cannot escape them. Yet, even when our situation seems desolate, God sows seeds of life and hope into our hearts. No matter how impossible something seems, we are not without the promise of renewal. As long as we live, we can depend on God's ability to redeem the most hopeless situation.

Maybe you're in the middle of a harsh winter, or maybe you're just beginning to see the first signs of spring. Whether your trial seems endless or is finally changing, God is worthy of your praise. As difficult as it is, you can lift up his name in the middle of the darkest night. There is no suffering that lasts forever. Even when your endurance is tested, you can trust that new life will come. There is renewal on the horizon.

Redeemer, I trust that you are in control. Hold me close as I endure through trials. You will redeem what is lost. Renew my hope and fill my heart with peace.

Raw Emotions

In the multitude of my anxieties within me,
Your comforts delight my soul.

PSALM 94:19 NKJV

King David was known as a man after God's own heart. He did not hold back his feelings from God. His praise is filled with raw emotion and honest declarations. When we pray, we can follow David's example. There is no need to clean up our words or attempt to present a perfect picture to God. He will never reject us for saying the wrong thing or shame us for sharing our true feelings.

When you truly bear your soul to God, you leave room for him to move in your life. You cannot properly stitch up a wound that is covered in layers of bandages. In the same way, God can't properly heal the broken parts of your heart if you refuse to acknowledge they are there. Don't let shame or fear get in the way of the complete and thorough healing God has for you. When you are vulnerable with him, he will meet you with power and faithfulness.

God, you are my comforter and my safe place. I don't want to hold anything back from you. Teach me how to be honest and authentic before you. I trust you for healing and new life.

WHAT REMAINS

The words "once again" clearly show us that everything that
was made—things that can be shaken—will be destroyed.
Only the things that cannot be shaken will remain.

HEBREWS 12:27 NCV

As we get closer to Jesus' return, everything will be
shaken. We don't know when, and we don't know exactly
what it will look like, but Scripture is clear that there will be a
great reckoning. Anything eternal will remain standing, but
everything else will crumble. We find security in belonging
to the kingdom of Heaven. No matter what happens, God's
people will not be destroyed. We know without a doubt that
God will hold us steadily in his hands.

Build your life upon the foundation of Jesus who never
fails or falters. He will keep you safe no matter what is going
on around you. There is no need to be afraid of what is to
come because God has promised redemption and perfection
for all who look to him for salvation. Grasp hold of what is
eternal and let go of everything that will not last. Even when
everything else falls away, God's love will be strong.

*Lord, help me build my life upon the unshakable things of
your kingdom. When the world is shaking, keep me firmly
rooted in your love. Give me the perseverance to endure to the
end. I want to spend eternity with you.*

He Is There

Even though the Lord may allow you
to go through a season of hardship and difficulty,
he himself will be there with you.
He will not hide himself from you,
for your eyes will constantly see him as your Teacher.

ISAIAH 30:20 TPT

It can be discouraging to experience seasons of hardship and difficulty. Nobody wants to experience pain, loss, or devastation. Even when we suffer, God's goodness is present. He does not leave us to navigate hardships on our own. He continues to comfort, teach, and guide us, even when it means carrying us because our knees have buckled, and our strength is gone.

God is with you. He is not absent from your suffering. He will not hide himself when you are in pain, and he will not ignore your cries for help. He knows exactly how to comfort you and how to lead you forward. He is with you when you feel strong and when you cannot take another step. Invite him to walk with you through the trials you are dealing with. Allow his presence to bring you peace and relief.

God, bind up my wounds and strengthen me with your love. When I am weak, I will trust in your strength. I need your help and your comfort. You are the only one who can see me through.

Keep On Growing

I pray this: that your love will keep on growing in knowledge and every kind of discernment.

PHILIPPIANS 1:9 CSB

As long as we live, we can continue to grow in wisdom. God has an unlimited supply, and he is extravagantly generous. He is eager to give good gifts to his children. If we desire to grow in love, he will do it. If we want to gain further knowledge and discernment, he will do it. He is not bothered by our requests. He loves to teach us his ways and show us what is best. As we follow him, we will see that there is no limit to the growth we can experience in his presence.

May you know the transformative power of God's love in your life. May you seek to continually expand in your ability to love others well. You may reach your own limits over and over again, but God doesn't have any. If you want to grow in love, there is never a stopping point. You won't be held back by money, location, intellect, or time. If loving well is your goal, nothing stands in your way.

Lord, I want to grow in love. Please give me knowledge and discernment as I follow you. Expand my understanding and help me love others like you do.

Good News

Like cold water to a weary soul
is good news from a distant land.

PROVERBS 25:25 NIV

Good news can revive a weary soul and bring relief to
a worried heart. When the world seems dark and there is
chaos around every corner, it can be difficult to see what is
good. Small acts of kindness shine brightly, and glimpses
of redemption bring hope to our weary souls. We see
destruction and desolation everywhere we look, yet God is
still at work.

Look to the Lord today and ask him to remind you of
what is good. If you've been focusing on the world's hurt
and pain, you may feel discouraged or hopeless. Lift your
eyes and let your Maker give you hope. No matter how dark
things seem, better days are coming. No matter how horrible
the world becomes, keep your hope steadily in the perfection
of God. He has encouragement for your challenges, hope
for your despair, and his love will cover the cracks of your
disappointment. God is exceptionally good, and his presence
brings light and life to all.

*God, I long for a dose of good news today. Please speak to my
heart. Thank you for the power of your love which meets me
every day. Keep my eyes steadily on you and fill me with hope.*

Skillful Potter

Now, O Lord, you are our Father;
we are the clay, and you are our potter;
we are all the work of your hand.

ISAIAH 64:8 ESV

We are like clay in the hands of a potter. God is molding each of us into something beautiful. Our lives are a testimony of his goodness and a reflection of his love. If we stay humble and soft-hearted, we will experience the goodness of his plans for us. There is no need to resist his work in our lives because he knows what is best. Everything he does has a purpose and is meant for our good.

God loves you deeply. His work in your life reflects that love. As you look to him for guidance, he will lead you along the best path. He knows what you need, and he knows exactly how to equip you. You can confidently follow his voice because he will not lead you astray. Even though you might not understand exactly what he is doing in your life, you can trust that he has good things in store for you. Partner with him today and trust that he will take care of you.

God, I trust you because I know your nature. You are kind, loving, true, and just. Thank you for taking care of me. Continue to shape my life and help me honor you in all I do.

Patiently Waiting

Wait patiently for the LORD.
Be brave and courageous.
Yes, wait patiently for the LORD.

PSALM 27:14 NLT

God knows exactly what he is doing. He is not at the mercy of worldly circumstances or human timelines. He will be faithful because he is strong enough to carry out all of his plans. There is nothing holding him back. All his promises will come to pass. We know this to be true, so we can wait patiently and full of expectation. We don't wait without hope.

God won't always move how you expect him to. Just because you don't understand a situation doesn't mean God isn't at work. He asks you to be brave and to wait patiently. You can do this with full confidence because you know that God is reliable and true to his Word. He doesn't ask you to do anything without merit. He will come through. Trust in his goodness and continue to seek his face.

Lord, I need your help in seasons of waiting. Help me be confident even when I don't understand your plans. Keep my eyes on you as I surrender control of my life. I trust you will be faithful.

God with Us

"The virgin will be pregnant. She will have a son, and they
will name him Immanuel," which means "God with us."

MATTHEW 1:23 NCV

God can do anything he wants with his creation. As the
Maker, he has full authority to do as he pleases. With every
option imaginable at his disposal, he chose to come and dwell
among us. He sent his Son to put on flesh and be confined
to humanity. Jesus came so we could be reconciled and
redeemed because God longs for communion with his people.

From the very beginning, God has desired to be with
you. You are his child, and he wants to be near you. He is
delighted by your existence. His love for you is so great that
he sacrificed part of himself to save you. You will never know
a love deeper or more expansive than God's. Jesus is the
embodiment of that love. He is living proof that God wants
to be with you.

Immanuel, thank you for humbling yourself and coming to
save me. Thank you for showing me how much the Father
loves me. I am so grateful for your life and your sacrifice.

Long-Awaited Messiah

A child is born to us,
a son is given to us.
The government will rest on his shoulders.
And he will be called:
Wonderful Counselor, Mighty God,
Everlasting Father, Prince of Peace.

Isaiah 9:6 nlt

God is constantly showing up in unexpected ways. He rarely operates the way we think he will. This was especially true when Jesus came to earth. Everyone expected a lofty king and a powerful ruler. The long-awaited Messiah was supposed to save them from their enemies and bring salvation at last. No one expected that position to be filled by a helpless baby. God's kingdom does not operate according to our expectations.

Embrace Jesus as the gift he was intended to be. Let him rule and reign in your life with full authority. There is no need to hesitate to give him control. He is the embodiment of God's goodness. He is a perfect counselor and a bringer of peace. Trust your Savior and rejoice in God's perfect plan.

Jesus, I am so thankful for you. Thank you for the humble way you came to earth. I trust you for my salvation.

Powerful and Strong

The word of God is alive and powerful. It is sharper than the sharpest two-edged sword, cutting between soul and spirit, join and marrow.

HEBREWS 4:12 NKJV

God's Word is powerful and strong. It is the most valuable tool we have been given. His Word teaches us how to do his will and strengthens us when we are weak. It encourages us, guides us, and draws us closer to God's heart. As we study his Word, we learn more about his character, and we build a foundation of trust in our relationship with him. The more we hide his promises in our hearts, the more equipped we are to follow him for all our days.

Life can quickly become chaotic, and it's easy to push aside the discipline of reading God's Word. Take time today to be refreshed by Scripture. You can read it, listen to it, sing it, or talk about it with others. No matter how you consume it, let the roots of truth grow deep into your heart. Let God's Word wash over you and have its full effect in your life.

God, thank you for your Word. Help me consume it every change I get. Fill my heart with truth and teach me more about you. I want the power of your Word to be at work in my life.

COUNTLESS MIRACLES

LORD my God, you have done many miracles.
Your plans for us are many.
If I tried to tell them all,
there would be too many to count.

PSALM 40:5 NCV

The miracles of God cannot be counted. We are surrounded by evidence of his goodness. We live in a culture that glorifies instant gratification and the constant search for personal satisfaction. We are so focused on our own lives that we rarely look up and take notice of the world around us. If we pay attention, we will see God's gracious hand everywhere we look. We'll see it in creation, in our own stories, and in the lives of those around us. God has done great things for all of us.

When the world seems dark, grasp ahold of every testimony of God's goodness you can find. Rejoice over the smallest miracle and soak in every ray of light you see. Devote your life to noticing the way God moves. You will never run out of content. Turn your heart toward him in worship and be encouraged by all he has done. As you deliberately seek the hand of God, your confidence will be bolstered by his faithfulness.

Marvelous One, thank you for all you have done and have yet to do. Help me see your goodness everywhere I go.

What Is Good

Dear friend, do not imitate what is evil, but what is good. The one who does good is of God; the one who does evil has not seen God.

3 John 1:11 csb

God's way is simple, though it is not always easy. When we choose to imitate what is good, we choose to be loving, kind, and generous. We reflect God's character and show the world what he is really like. As we seek to be like him, he transforms us from the inside out. We become like what we emulate.

Even when it's inconvenient, you are called to be an imitator of God. He has given you an example to follow and it's in your best interest to do it. Not only has he set a standard of living, but he has also equipped you with everything you need. Furthermore, even when you miss the mark, you will be met with gracious kindness and faithful love. God doesn't ask you to imitate him and then expect you to do it perfectly. His grace does not waver in the face of your flaws.

God, lead me on the path of your goodness. Help me choose the right thing, even when it is difficult. I want to be more like you. Thank you for the grace you've given me.

Sow Peace

Peacemakers who sow in peace
reap a harvest of righteousness.

JAMES 3:18 NIV

It isn't extremely popular to pursue peace. Our culture
loves to be contrary, to shout our opinions from the
rooftops, and to fight over who is right. Even so, Christ calls
us to seek peace. He wants us to lay down our weapons, not
to take them up. Jesus rebuked Peter for cutting off the ear
of a guard who had come to take him away. Christ reached
out and healed the guard's ear, and then he did not resist his
arrest or the horror that would follow.

Scripture promises if you pursue peace, you will reap
a harvest of righteousness. Ask God what this might look
like in your life. It might mean quieting your heart and
guarding your words. It might mean seeking reconciliation
when you would rather engage in a conflict. It might mean
encouraging others to step back and trust God's plans rather
than seeking vindication. As you seek peace in your own life,
it will overflow to those around you.

*Prince of Peace, I want to follow your example. Help me
choose peace over vengeance. Help me create peace wherever I
go. Give me a calm spirit and an unshakeable trust in you.*

Train to Listen

Train your heart to listen when I speak
and open your spirit wide to expand
your discernment—
then pass it on to your sons and daughters.

PROVERBS 2:2 TPT

When we train our hearts to listen to God's voice, we open ourselves up to a wealth of wisdom. God's wisdom teaches us to walk in understanding, peace, and love. It teaches us to do good when no one else does. Wisdom follows God's ways even when they are unconventional, uncomfortable, or inconvenient. Through wisdom, we learn to be humble and teachable because we know there is always room to grow.

Listen for God's voice, and he will reveal himself to you. He will direct your steps and give you confidence as you follow him. You don't have to struggle to figure out what is right and wrong. Under his guidance, you can trust that he is in control and won't lead you astray. Get to know his voice by spending time in prayer, reading the Word, and learning from other believers. The more familiar you become with his ways, the easier it is to recognize his prompting.

God, I want to be familiar with your voice. Teach me your ways and fill me with wisdom. Give me grace to follow you closely. I want to walk with you all of my days.

ALWAYS AT WORK

"I am about to do something new.
See, I have already begun! Do you not see it?
I will make a pathway through the wilderness.
I will create rivers in the dry wasteland."

ISAIAH 43:19 NLT

God is always at work. Whether or not we are paying attention, he is always moving. He is redeeming hearts, directing footsteps, and making pathways through the wilderness. He is faithfully keeping his promises, and he is taking care of his children with compassion and tenderness. He sees each of our lives as a whole, and he is weaving our days together into a masterpiece.

As the year ends, you may be considering all that lies ahead. It is good to take time to remember what God has already done. As you dream about what lies ahead, don't forget how God has been faithful in your life. He has carried you all of your days, and he will not forsake you now. He already knows what tomorrow will look like. Trust in the plans he has for you.

Lord, thank you for all the ways you've shown up this year. You have been so faithful to me. I look to you for direction and guidance. Lead me forward on the path you've chosen for me.